The Complete
AFRICAN-AMERICAN
BABY CHECKLIST

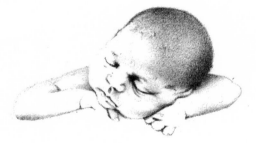

The Complete
AFRICAN-AMERICAN
BABY CHECKLIST

A Total Organizing System

ELYSE ZORN KARLIN and DAISY SPIER with DIANE WILLIAMS

Illustrated by Fredericka Ribes

AVON BOOKS ◆ NEW YORK

This book is not intended for the purpose of parental diagnosis or medical treatment of children. Parents of children with specific health concerns should discuss these concerns with their pediatricians. Before starting a child on any diet or eating program, or before altering a doctor-prescribed eating program, parents should discuss the intended diet with their pediatrician. Although every effort has been made to include the most current information in this book, there can be no guarantee that this information won't change with time.

AVON BOOKS, INC.
1350 Avenue of the Americas
New York, New York 10019

Text copyright © 1999 by Elyse Zorn Karlin and Daisy Spier
Cover and interior illustrations © 1999 by Fredericka Ribes
Interior design by Stanley S. Drate / Folio Graphics Co. Inc.
Published by arrangement with the authors
ISBN: 0-380-80006-3
www.avonbooks.com

First Avon Books Trade Paperback Printing: March 1999

AVON TRADEMARK REG. U.S. PAT. OFF. AND IN OTHER COUNTRIES, MARCA REGISTRADA, HECHO EN U.S.A.

Printed in the U.S.A.

OPM   10   9   8   7   6   5   4   3   2   1

"There is nothing as ancient as infancy. Unchanging ancientness is born into homes again and again in the form of a baby, yet the freshness, beauty, innocence and sweetness it had at the beginning of history is the same today."

—Rabindranath Tagore, *Folk Literature*

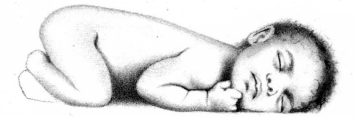

CONTENTS

Preface   xiii

How to Use *The Complete African-American
Baby Checklist*   xv

Part One

A HEALTHY PREGNANCY

Medical Issues to Consider Early in Your Pregnancy   5

Guidelines for Taking Care of Yourself and Your
  Unborn Baby   7

Your Early Pregnancy Checklist   8

Record of Prenatal Medical Appointments   9

What to Ask Your HMO/Managed Care/Insurance
  Provider about Maternity Benefits   10

What to Ask Your HMO/Managed Care/Insurance
  Provider about Baby's Coverage   12

Medical Facts African-American Mothers-to-Be Should
  Know   14

Part Two

PREPARING FOR BABY'S ARRIVAL

Last-Trimester Checklist   22

Last-Month Checklist   25

Layette Checklist   27

Preparing-the-Nursery Checklist   29

Choosing a Name   30

Name Worksheet—First Name   31

Name Worksheet—Middle Name   32

Announcement List   33

Guest List for Religious/Nonreligious Ceremony or
    Naming Ceremony   35

Gift/Thank-You Note Checklist   37

Hospital Checklist   39

Hospital Call List   41

Checklist for Partner, Friend, or Family Member   43

Single Motherhood   46

Resources for Single Mothers   47

Part Three

BUYING EQUIPMENT AND CLOTHING

Babies Don't Need Brand-New Everything   54

Guidelines for Choosing Equipment   56

Guidelines for Buying Children's Clothing   62

Equipment/Clothing Loan Record   64

Guidelines for Choosing Diapers   66

Information about Car Seats   69

Information about Strollers and Carriages   71

Day Outing Checklist   74

Overnight Checklist   76

Age-Appropriate Toys   77

Part Four

HEALTH MAINTENANCE

Pediatrician Interview Form   84

First Aid Medical Supply Checklist   86

Essential Phone Numbers   87

What You Should Know about African-American
    Children and Asthma   88

Record of Allergies and Reactions   90

What You Should Know about Sickle-Cell Anemia and
    African-American Babies   92

Special Considerations for African-American Skin and
    Hair   94

Infant/Toddler Development Chart   96

Record of Baby's Height and Weight   98

Baby's Achievements   99

Record of Baby's Teeth   100

Record of Dental Visits   101

Schedule of Immunizations and Reactions   102

Record of Immunizations   104

Medical/Dental Insurance Record   105

When to Let Your Infant/Toddler Return to Day Care
    or Play Group   107

Part Five

FEEDING

Bottle-Feeding Tracking Form   113

Breast-Feeding Tracking Form   115

Food Introduction Record   117

Lactose Intolerance in Children   119

Information about Formula   121

Information about Baby Bottles and Nipples   123

Mother's Exercise Record   125

Homemade Baby Food   127

Baby Food Recipes   128

Children and Ethnic Foods   129

Grocery List   131

Part Six

SELECTING AND EVALUATING CHILD CARE

Adult Caregiver Interview Form   *139*

Day Care Center or Preschool Evaluation Form   *142*

Interview Form for Choosing Home-Based Child Care   *145*

Child Care Resources   *149*

Teenage Baby-sitter Interview Form   *151*

Baby-sitter Instruction Sheet   *153*

Baby-sitter Directory   *155*

Part Seven

BUYING BY MAIL ORDER

Tips for Buying by Mail Order   *160*

Mail Order Purchasing Record   *161*

Mail Order Resources   *165*

Part Eight

RESOURCES

Organizations   *196*

Magazines and Newsletters   *207*

Useful Information as Your Child Grows   *209*

Boarding Schools and Camps for African-American
  Children   *211*

Resources on Adoption   *213*

Parents' Groups and Preschool Activities Record   *214*

Child's Friends and Their Parents   *218*

About the Authors   *223*

PREFACE

"My family directly and my people indirectly
have given me the kind of strength that enables
me to go anywhere."

—Maya Angelou, American writer, poet, and actress

True or false?

- Black women are twice as likely as white women to develop gestational diabetes during pregnancy.
- Black children are more prone to asthma than other children.
- "Gripe water" contains an ingredient that may not be safe for baby.
- African-American women burn calories more slowly at rest than white women.

All of these statements are true. To be honest, we couldn't answer all of them correctly either before we began researching this book.

About ten years ago, we began gathering information for a book to help pregnant women and new mothers get organized during the chaotic period of pregnancy and babyhood (*The Complete Baby Checklist: A Total Organizing System for New Parents*, Avon Books, 1992). We set out to develop a practical system that would help expectant and new parents organize all the tasks and details that pregnancy and a baby bring into their lives. We focused on the dynamics of organizing this blessed event and its consequences and on creating an orderly life for a new mother. Our goal was to develop a tool to help parents cope better. We didn't focus on how family history and ethnic background might affect what happens in your pregnancy, in the birth of your child, and in a child's first few years of life.

When our editor, Charlotte Abbott, came to us and suggested we consider writing a new verion of *The Complete Baby Checklist: A Total Organizing System for New Parents*—one specifically for African-American parents—we weren't certain how to respond. We wondered how this book would be any different from our original book.

Yet, the more we thought about it, the more we read, the more we realized that this new book made absolute sense. There are medical, cultural, and familial issues that are different for African-American women during pregnancy and for their babies.

When we sat down to write *The Complete African-American Baby Checklist* we decided not to ''throw the baby out with the bathwater.'' We didn't discard our original manuscript and start all over. We took the information that all new parents could benefit from and added to that the knowledge we felt was relevant to African-American parents. The result was this book, which we hope will offer you an opportunity to share our best parent-organizing knowledge as well as information on important medical, health, educational, and other issues pertinent to black families. Our goal was to help you get organized with your new baby and to celebrate the unique experience of African-American parenthood. We hope we have succeeded!

How to Use
The Complete African-American Baby Checklist

T his book is divided into eight sections. At the beginning of each section is a description of the organizing forms and charts and how to use them. Start by familiarizing yourself with each of the sections. If you're awaiting baby's arrival, you can start using Parts One and Two immediately, and parts of some of the other sections as well. If you do, you'll have a head start on being organized when baby arrives.

Some of the forms in this book are intended for use outside the home. In most cases you can just take this book with you and use the forms right in the book. However, for some forms, such as the grocery shopping list, which you'll want to use over and over again, it might be wise to make some photocopies so you'll have unlimited usage. We think the forms and lists are helpful as they are, but everybody is different. So feel free to change or adapt them to suit your needs.

Keep the book in a handy place so it is accessible to everyone who will take care of baby—Mom, Dad, partner, caregiver, grandparents, and so forth. Try keeping it in the kitchen, or in the room where you spend the most time.

The Complete African-American Baby Checklist is primarily meant to be used from pregnancy throughout the first year of baby's life. However, many of the forms and much of the information will continue to be useful through the later years. Simply refer to the Contents to find the help you need.

Part One

A HEALTHY PREGNANCY

"A child must learn early to believe that he is somebody worthwhile and that he can do many praiseworthy things. The baby must be made to know that he or she is wanted."

—Benjamin Mays, "What Man Lives By"

I t seems as if the minute you discover you are pregnant, you realize there are many new things to learn about and many things to do. What should you do first? Pregnancy is a happy and healthy state, and your body was designed for it. One of the most important things you can do is eat right to take care of yourself and your unborn baby. Even if your pregnancy appears perfectly normal, it is important to get medical care throughout it. The following checklists will help guide you through a healthy pregnancy:

Medical Issues to Consider Early in Your Pregnancy

Covers medical considerations such as selecting a medical caregiver, family medical history, and genetic testing.

Guidelines for Taking Care of Yourself and Your Unborn Baby

Provides tips on how to minimize health risks during pregnancy.

Your Early Pregnancy Checklist

Helps you get started with regard to new issues to consider, such as medical insurance, savings, maternity clothes, notes on your pregnancy, and so forth.

Record of Prenatal Medical Appointments

Use this chart to keep a record of your medical appointments and the questions you want to ask your doctor/midwife.

What to Ask Your HMO/Managed Care/Insurance Provider about Maternity Benefits

Medical insurance and medical plans have become very complicated and difficult to understand. Here are all the questions you need to ask about your benefits, and suggestions about what to do if you are not insured or a member of an HMO. Medical care is expensive. Be prepared by asking all these questions.

What to Ask Your HMO/Managed Care/Insurance Provider about Baby's Coverage

These questions will help you understand what medical coverage your baby will have.

Medical Facts African-American Mothers-to-Be Should Know

Here you will find what medical issues are particularly important for black pregnant women.

Medical Issues to Consider Early in Your Pregnancy

▨ As soon as you know you are pregnant or suspect you might be pregnant, make an appointment with your doctor and/or midwife. It's important to meet with your doctor as early as possible in your pregnancy. This is the time to decide whether you would prefer to have an obstetrician and/or a midwife for pregnancy care and delivery. Research the benefits of each.

▨ If you or someone in your family has a history of medical problems such as high blood pressure, diabetes, sickle-cell anemia, asthma, or lupus, it is critical to let your obstetrician know right away so that he/she can provide you with the proper care. Certain medical conditions are more likely to occur in black people and can cause complications during pregnancy.

According to a Northwestern University study, gestational diabetes is nearly two times more likely in black women than white women.

Blacks are in a higher risk group for high blood pressure, asthma, and lupus.

Sickle-cell anemia occurs primarily in blacks.

▨ If you have an infectious disease or a sexually transmitted disease, be sure to tell your doctor.

5 ⌒

■ You and your mate should be tested for the sickle-cell trait even if you don't have sickle-cell anemia, since you may be carriers of the disease and pass it on to your child. (Both parents must carry the trait to pass on the disease.) Whether you are considering having a baby or are pregnant, talk to your doctor about genetic testing and counseling for sickle-cell anemia and other hereditary conditions blacks are more prone to, such as G6PD deficiency, a rare blood disorder affecting males but for which women are the carriers.

■ Set up regularly scheduled medical appointments.

GUIDELINES FOR TAKING CARE OF YOURSELF AND YOUR UNBORN BABY

F ollow these guidelines throughout your pregnancy to minimize health risks for you and your baby and lessen the chances of premature birth:

- Do not take any drugs or medicines, either prescription or nonprescription, without your doctor's approval. Do not use any illegal drugs.
- Do not drink wine, beer, or any other alcoholic beverages.
- Do not smoke while you are pregnant.
- Eat a balanced diet.
- Get enough calcium in your diet.
- Take multivitamins with folic acid.*
- Follow your doctor's recommendations.

*Doctors are now recommending that women of child-bearing age take folic acid daily to help prevent neural tube problems such as spina bifida.

Your Early Pregnancy Checklist

☐ **C**heck the pregnancy/maternity benefits offered by your medical insurance or HMO. (See page 12 for What to Ask Your HMO/Managed Care/Insurance Provider about Maternity Benefits.)

☐ **I**f you don't have medical insurance, check services provided by clinics at your local hospital. Call your local or state social services department for information.

☐ **B**egin a savings account or add to an existing savings account to cover your increased expenses once the baby is born.

☐ **T**o save money, borrow maternity or larger size clothing from friends. Consider sewing your own maternity clothes. Simplicity Pattern Company has a nice array of patterns that are fashionable, easy to sew, and available in many sizes.

☐ **C**heck maternity/paternity leave policies offered by your employer.

☐ **A**frican-American history has traditionally been passed on orally from generation to generation. Start a written history for your baby. (Consider purchasing *Grandmother's Gift of Memories* by Danita Green or similar books.)

☐ **C**hart a family tree.

☐ **K**eep notes on your pregnancy—a diary of your emotions, your health, your dreams.

RECORD OF PRENATAL MEDICAL APPOINTMENTS

Date/Time	Doctor/ Midwife	Doctor's/Midwife's Comments
_____	_____	_____
_____	_____	_____
_____	_____	_____
_____	_____	_____
_____	_____	_____
_____	_____	_____
_____	_____	_____
_____	_____	_____
_____	_____	_____

Write questions for your doctor or midwife here:

_____

_____

_____

_____

_____

WHAT TO ASK YOUR HMO/ MANAGED CARE/INSURANCE PROVIDER ABOUT MATERNITY BENEFITS

I t is important to tell your provider that you are pregnant as soon as you find out. Many providers require
you to be precertified for maternity benefits.

Ask Them the Following Questions

■ Now that I am pregnant, what steps do I have to go
through to get all my benefits?

_____

_____

■ Do I have a choice between a doctor and/or a midwife?
At what stage of my pregnancy do I have to choose?

_____

_____

■ How many maternity visits do you recommend and how
many will I be covered for?

_____

_____

■ What prenatal testing will you cover? Blood testing for
genetic and other diseases? Sonograms? Amniocentesis?
Other?

_____

_____

■ **W**hat provisions do you have for high-risk pregnancies?

_____

_____

■ **D**o you offer/cover child-birthing classes?

_____

_____

■ **W**hat hospital or birthing facility is covered under my plan?

_____

_____

■ **H**ow long can I stay in the hospital after the baby is born? Is your policy different for vaginal versus cesarean-section deliveries? What if there are complications?

_____

_____

■ **W**hat if I have to be hospitalized during my pregnancy?

_____

_____

■ **I**s there anything with regard to prenatal and postnatal care that I should be aware of that you do not cover?

_____

_____

■ **P**lease explain in detail what I will be expected to pay for myself.

_____

_____

WHAT TO ASK YOUR HMO/ MANAGED CARE/INSURANCE PROVIDER ABOUT BABY'S COVERAGE

▓ Is the newborn's first in-hospital examination covered?

_____

_____

▓ What in-hospital lab tests are covered?

_____

_____

▓ Is circumcision covered? Must it be done by a physician?

_____

_____

▓ Will there by any home care follow-up by a nurse?

_____

_____

▓ Do I have my choice of pediatrician?

_____

_____

▓ Can the baby be seen by the same pediatrician for every checkup?

_____

_____

- If the baby needs to see a specialist, do I have to get a referral from the pediatrician? Do I need to get approval from the HMO/Managed Care/Insurance Company?

_____

_____

- How many well-baby visits (checkups) is my child covered for in the first year?

_____

_____

- How many well-baby visits is my child covered for in the second year?

_____

_____

- What is the well-child coverage once my baby is two years old?

_____

_____

- Will the insurance pay for baby's immunizations?

_____

_____

- What lab tests are covered?

_____

_____

- Are X rays covered? What other diagnostic tests are covered?

_____

_____

Medical Facts African-American Mothers-to-Be Should Know

■ Calcium is an important nutrient during pregnancy. Seventy-five percent of black Americans are lactose intolerant, meaning they have difficulty digesting milk and milk products.

> If you are lactose intolerant, be sure to discuss this with your doctor. Your baby needs calcium to build strong bones and you do, too.

> Lactose-free products are available, such as Lactaid milk and Lactaid tablets, to help you digest the milk.

> If you can't drink enough milk or eat enough dairy products, you should supplement your diet with foods high in calcium such as salmon, sardines, broccoli, kale, turnip greens, collard greens, and chickpeas.

■ If you have sickle-cell anemia (1 percent of African-Americans have the disease), you will have to be watched carefully during your pregnancy, to avoid serious complications and for your baby's well-being.

> Be sure your doctor is experienced with sickle-cell so he/she can guide you through a safe pregnancy.

> If you and the child's father were not tested for this trait before or during pregnancy, your baby should be tested within a few days of his/her birth.

■ If you are diabetic you must take extra care of yourself during pregnancy to ensure you and your baby's health. Speak to a diabetes specialist about your pregnancy.

You will have to keep your blood sugar levels in tight control.

You may have to make adjustments in your diet and test your glucose level more frequently.

If you have Type I diabetes you may have different or extra insulin requirements.

If you have Type II diabetes, a condition with a higher incidence among blacks than whites, you may be switched from oral medications to insulin.

■ Even if you are not diabetic, you may get gestational diabetes, a type of diabetes that develops in 2 to 5 percent of pregnant women and, in most cases, disappears once the baby is born. It may recur at a later time.

Black women are twice as likely to develop this type of diabetes than white women. A glucose tolerance test, usually given in the second trimester, can determine whether you have gestational diabetes.

To control the amount of sugar in your blood, and ensure that your body is converting the carbohydrates you eat into usable energy for you and your baby, you will have to watch your diet carefully and you may need insulin.

Women with gestational diabetes may have very large babies, if the diabetes is not controlled. There may be increased risk of fetal distress and injury to the baby during childbirth. In addition the child may suffer from low blood sugar at birth which may result in neurological damage.

■ **O**besity (which is also higher in black women) and diabetes may lead to high blood pressure and heart disease.

■ *Preeclampsia* (toxemia), high blood pressure induced by pregnancy, is a rare condition that can become very serious if not monitored and controlled carefully. Pregnant women with preeclampsia retain water and show the presence of protein in the urine and toxins in the blood. High blood pressure is more likely to occur in black women during pregnancy; therefore, it is important to be under a doctor's care to avoid any negative effects it can have on you and your baby's health.

Follow doctor's directions with regard to medications, diet, exercise, and rest.

Part Two

PREPARING FOR BABY'S ARRIVAL

"A newborn baby is an extraordinary event; and I have never seen two babies who looked exactly alike. Here is the breathing miracle who could not live an instant without you, with a skull more fragile than an egg, a miracle of eyes, legs, toenails and lungs."

—James Baldwin, *No Name in the Street*

T he last trimester of pregnancy passes quickly. Suddenly you realize that there's a lot to do before the baby is born. The same is true if you're awaiting a baby through adoption.

To help you feel more organized in preparing for baby's arrival, we've created a number of checklists for Mom and Dad. Of course, many items included are subject to personal preference. You certainly don't have to buy or do *everything* on these lists, but they should be helpful in making certain nothing important is forgotten.

Last-Trimester Checklist

Includes items that require lead time to order, do, or select.

Last-Month Checklist

Covers those last-minute details you may forget as you become excited and anxious about baby's arrival.

Layette Checklist

This is a list of the basic items of clothing and linens you'll need for your new baby. We've used minimum amounts here. If you want to do laundry less often, you can opt to buy more, but keep in mind how quickly babies outgrow their clothes.

Preparing the Nursery

Here's everything you need for baby's room.

Choosing a Name

A name lasts a lifetime—this section will help you focus on making a choice that really fits your baby and reflects your African-American heritage.

Name Worksheets

During the months that you are waiting for baby, jot down your favorite names, and narrow the list down to your first choice.

Announcement List

You'll be too busy to draw up an announcement list after baby arrives, so do it beforehand if you can.

Guest List for Religious/NonReligious Ceremony or Naming Ceremony

If you're planning to have a christening, you should plan your guest list before baby is born. Select guests from your announcement list.

Gift/Thank-You Note Checklist

It's wonderful—there are baby showers before, and visitors bearing gifts after. But you're so tired and busy, it's difficult to remember who gave which gift and whether you sent a thank-you note. Use this list to avoid embarrassing errors.

Hospital Checklist

The last thing you want to do is to start looking for all these things to take with you when you go into labor. Pack two to four weeks before your due date.

Hospital Call List

Names and numbers will help Mom and Dad remember to call everyone and keep track of who has not been reached with the happy news of baby's arrival.

Checklist for Partner, Friend, or Family Member

Dad has a lot to do while Mom is in the hospital. This list will help him remember everything.

Single Motherhood

Being a parent is all-consuming, but even more so when you're a single parent. Here are some suggestions for how to get the help you'll need.

Resources for Single Mothers

A list of organizations that provide information and help for single mothers.

Last-Trimester Checklist

☐ **B**egin buying the layette. If you're uncomfortable with having these items at home in advance of baby's birth, many stores will hold them aside for you.

☐ **S**ign up for childbirth classes. Ask your doctor or hospital for recommendations. Investigate Bradley versus Lamaze method and others.

☐ **D**etermine who will be your childbirth coach. This can be your partner, a friend, or a relative, but be certain they are willing to accompany you to all the childbirth classes (if you take classes) as well as be there for the birth.

☐ **C**heck your insurance coverage for well-baby care and your own hospitalization. Many insurance companies now insist they be notified in advance.

☐ **S**tart looking at baby announcements.

☐ **T**hink about buying a good camera and/or video camera if you don't have one. Keep in mind that some hospitals forbid the use of flashes in the delivery room, and choose your camera accordingly.

☐ **S**tart looking through mail order catalogs for any items you might want to order.

☐ **R**ead about breast-feeding and be prepared for any problems. You may also want to discuss it with your doctor or attend a few meetings of the La Leche League, an organization that promotes breast-feeding. There should be a local chapter in your area.

☐ **A**rrange details of your maternity leave with your employer.

☐ **R**egister with hospital/birthing center where you will deliver baby. Some doctors may do this for you on request.

☐ **D**iscuss your anesthesia options with an anesthesiologist at the hospital.

☐ **I**nterview pediatricians. (See the forms in Part Four.)

☐ **S**tart thinking of child care options. You might want to make some calls and begin interviewing caregivers or visiting day care centers.

☐ **B**egin painting, wallpapering, and carpeting baby's room. As exhausting as this may seem now, it will be more difficult to do once baby is here.

☐ **F**ind out which pieces of baby equipment and/or furniture friends and relatives will lend or give you. (See Preparing-the-Nursery Checklist and Guidelines for Choosing Equipment.) Order nursery furniture, custom quilts, and curtains early.

☐ **E**xplore diaper services. Compare prices, and check on frequency of delivery/pickup as well as options for cloth versus disposables.

☐ **I**f there are other children in the family, by now you have probably told them about the new baby. It's a good time to buy a book for siblings that discusses being a big brother or sister, and to check with your hospital to see if there are any special "sibling" classes to help prepare the older child for the baby and Mom's hospital stay. You might also have siblings help decorate and select items for baby's room.

LAST-MONTH CHECKLIST

☐ **S**tart addressing announcement envelopes. It will save you precious time later.

☐ **P**ay bills as they come in and keep correspondence up-to-date. You'll be surprised how fast these things pile up after baby arrives.

☐ **S**pend time having fun with Dad-to-be. Go out to dinner, movies, etc., as often as you can.

☐ **R**est and pamper yourself as much as possible. Now's the time to rent your favorite video, read that book you've always wanted to, and put your feet up.

☐ **P**ack your suitcase for the hospital; include clothes for baby.

☐ **B**egin reading books on care of new babies. (See page 44.)

☐ **M**ake list of people to call about baby's birth. (See Hospital Call List.)

☐ **C**ook double portions of meals and freeze the extras.

☐ **B**uy a supply of: diapers, cotton balls, cotton swabs, bottles, pacifiers, baby wipes, baby soap, baby shampoo, baby powder, petroleum jelly, diaper ointment.

☐ **B**uy nursing pads, sanitary napkins, Preparation H, Tucks (antiseptic pads), for your postpartum return.

☐ **M**ake arrangements for help after the birth of your baby. Check with family and friends, or arrange for a baby nurse if you're planning to have one.

☐ **P**rewash all the baby's clothes and linens with baby soap or detergent, e.g., Ivory Snow or Dreft.

☐ **M**ake a final decision about names.

☐ **D**ecide where baby will sleep when coming home from the hospital. Some parents prefer to keep the baby in their room for the first few weeks.

☐ **D**iscuss circumcision with your doctor and/or religious leader and get recommendations and references from friends.

☐ **T**ake sibling(s) to buy a gift for the new baby; and buy one for the sibling(s) to receive after the baby is born. Some parents like to say it's a gift from the new baby.

☐ **C**heck to see if the hospital will allow sibling(s) to visit the new baby.

☐ **D**ecide who will take care of the sibling(s) while Mom's in the hospital, and have a backup plan in the event labor is early or your first choice becomes unavailable.

LAYETTE CHECKLIST

☐ **"C**oming home from the hospital" outfit: something comfortable for baby to wear. In cold weather, also bring a bunting or heavy blanket. In warmer weather you may just need a light blanket.

☐ **U**ndershirts (4–7); Onesies or other snap-crotch type recommended because they do not ride up on baby.

☐ **F**lame-retardant stretchies or pajamas (4–7)

☐ **K**imonos/nightgowns (4–7)

☐ **O**ther "dressier" outfits for visitors or special outings (3–5)

☐ **H**ooded towels and washcloths (3)

☐ **R**eceiving blankets (3–5)

☐ **Q**uilts (2)

- ☐ **C**rib sheets (3)

- ☐ **B**umpers for crib

- ☐ **F**lannel-covered rubber sheets (2–3)

- ☐ **C**hanging-table covers (3)

- ☐ **C**radle or bassinet sheets, if using (2–3)

- ☐ **C**loth diapers (minimum of 50; if using disposables, buy 12–24 cloth diapers for burping and cleanups)

- ☐ **R**ubber pants or diaper covers if using cloth diapers (3–5)

- ☐ **S**weaters (2–3)

- ☐ **B**ibs (3–5)

- ☐ **S**ocks or bootees

- ☐ **S**easonal: snowsuit, hat, mittens, bunting, sun bonnet, sun-suits, bathing suits

- ☐ **R**ain poncho

PREPARING-THE-NURSERY CHECKLIS

- ☐ **D**resser
- ☐ **T**emporary bed or bassinet
- ☐ **R**ocking chair
- ☐ **C**rib
- ☐ **H**amper
- ☐ **Q**uilt and bumpers
- ☐ **L**amp/night light/dimmer
- ☐ **D**iaper pail
- ☐ **M**usic box
- ☐ **S**tain-proof carpeting
- ☐ **H**umidifier
- ☐ **C**hanging table
- ☐ **B**aby nail scissors or clippers

- ☐ **B**aby wipes (choose brand without alcohol)
- ☐ **B**aby powder
- ☐ **D**iaper cream
- ☐ **C**otton balls
- ☐ **T**hermometer
- ☐ **C**lock
- ☐ **B**aby comb and brush
- ☐ **N**ursery monitor/ intercom
- ☐ **B**aby carrier (can be combo/car seat)
- ☐ **D**iaper pail
- ☐ **B**aby bath

> ther would in Africa, he knew that the matter
> ng and serious reflection, for he knew that what a
> called would really influence the kind of person
> he or she became."

—Alex Haley, *Roots: The Saga of an American Family*

N aming the baby can be a particularly symbolic action for African-American families. Think about our history: we lost our "true" names, and the traditions that went along with them on the African continent. We then had to use the names of slaveholders or the names chosen by them.

Nowadays we have the opportunity to find a name we like. We can honor a family member, inspire a child with the name of a famous African-American, pick a traditional African name, use a Eurocentric name, or even create a unique name. These possibilities are covered in recent paperback books:

The African-American Baby Name Book, Teresa Norman (Berkley Publishing, $12.00)

The Complete Guide to African-American Baby Names, Linda Wolfe Keister (Signet, $6.99)

1001 African Names: First and Last Names from the African Continent, Julia Stewart (Citadel Press, $10.95)

Proud Heritage: 11,101 Names for Your African-American Baby, Elza Dinwiddie-Boyd (Avon Books, $5.99)

What to Name Your African-American Baby, Benjamin Faulkner (St. Martin's Press, $7.95)

Name Worksheet
First Name

TOP TEN CHOICES

Boy   *Girl*

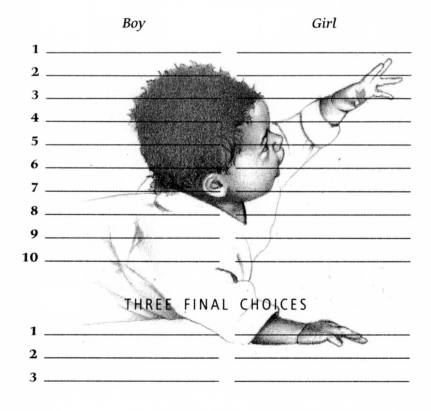

1 _____   _____
2 _____   _____
3 _____   _____
4 _____   _____
5 _____   _____
6 _____   _____
7 _____   _____
8 _____   _____
9 _____   _____
10 _____   _____

THREE FINAL CHOICES

1 _____   _____
2 _____   _____
3 _____   _____

FINAL CHOICE

_____   _____

NAME WORKSHEET
MIDDLE NAME

TOP TEN CHOICES

Boy   *Girl*

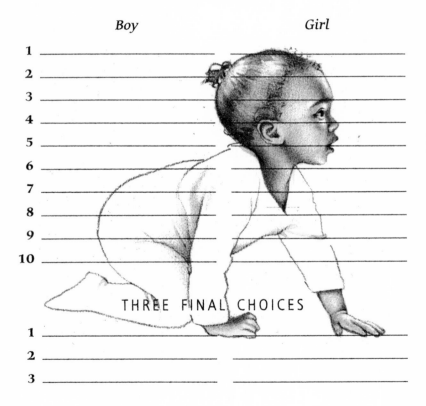

1 _____   _____
2 _____   _____
3 _____   _____
4 _____   _____
5 _____   _____
6 _____   _____
7 _____   _____
8 _____   _____
9 _____   _____
10 _____   _____

THREE FINAL CHOICES

1 _____   _____
2 _____   _____
3 _____   _____

FINAL CHOICE

_____   _____

Announcement List

Name and Address	Date Sent

Name and Address	Date Sent
_____	_____
_____	
_____	
_____	_____
_____	
_____	
_____	_____
_____	
_____	
_____	_____
_____	
_____	
_____	_____
_____	
_____	
_____	_____
_____	
_____	
_____	_____
_____	
_____	

Guest List for Religious/ Nonreligious Ceremony or Naming Ceremony

J ust as there has been a renewed interest in rites-of-passage and coming-of-age ceremonies, you may wish to consider a special naming celebration for your baby. For ideas and suggestions we recommend the book *For Every Season* by Barbara Eklof, which has ideas for African-American celebrations from traditional to contemporary.

Name	Relationship	Phone #	Attending Yes	No
			☐	☐
			☐	☐
			☐	☐
			☐	☐
			☐	☐
			☐	☐
			☐	☐
			☐	☐
			☐	☐
			☐	☐

	Name	Relationship	Phone #	Attending Yes	No
	_____	_____	_____	☐	☐
	_____	_____	_____	☐	☐
	_____	_____	_____	☐	☐
	_____	_____	_____	☐	☐
	_____	_____	_____	☐	☐
	_____	_____	_____	☐	☐
	_____	_____	_____	☐	☐
	_____	_____	_____	☐	☐
	_____	_____	_____	☐	☐
	_____	_____	_____	☐	☐
	_____	_____	_____	☐	☐
	_____	_____	_____	☐	☐
	_____	_____	_____	☐	☐
	_____	_____	_____	☐	☐
	_____	_____	_____	☐	☐
	_____	_____	_____	☐	☐
	_____	_____	_____	☐	☐
	_____	_____	_____	☐	☐
	_____	_____	_____	☐	☐
	_____	_____	_____	☐	☐

Gift/Thank-You Note Checklist

Gift Description	From	Date Received	Note Sent
_____	_____	_____	☐
_____	_____	_____	☐
_____	_____	_____	☐
_____	_____	_____	☐
_____	_____	_____	☐
_____	_____	_____	☐
_____	_____	_____	☐
_____	_____	_____	☐
_____	_____	_____	☐
_____	_____	_____	☐
_____	_____	_____	☐
_____	_____	_____	☐
_____	_____	_____	☐
_____	_____	_____	☐
_____	_____	_____	☐
_____	_____	_____	☐
_____	_____	_____	☐
_____	_____	_____	☐
_____	_____	_____	☐
_____	_____	_____	☐

Gift Description	From	Date Received	Note Sent
_____	_____	_____	☐
_____	_____	_____	☐
_____	_____	_____	☐
_____	_____	_____	☐
_____	_____	_____	☐
_____	_____	_____	☐
_____	_____	_____	☐
_____	_____	_____	☐
_____	_____	_____	☐
_____	_____	_____	☐
_____	_____	_____	☐
_____	_____	_____	☐
_____	_____	_____	☐
_____	_____	_____	☐
_____	_____	_____	☐
_____	_____	_____	☐
_____	_____	_____	☐
_____	_____	_____	☐
_____	_____	_____	☐

HOSPITAL CHECKLIST

- ☐ **I**nstruction sheets from childbirth classes and the "goody bag" they suggest for labor

- ☐ **P**retty nightgowns; nursing (or front-button) gowns optional (2)

- ☐ **B**athrobe and slippers

- ☐ **C**otton underpants (6)

- ☐ **N**ursing bras and nursing pads (3)

- ☐ **T**apes and cassettes or radio

- ☐ **C**ream for back massage

- ☐ **S**hampoo, hair dryer, soap, deodorant, toothpaste, toothbrush, cosmetics, and perfume

- ☐ **L**oose-fitting "coming home" clothes for Mom; pants will be more comfortable if they have elastic waistbands

- [ ] **L**ist of people (and phone numbers) to be called about baby's arrival

- [ ] **C**hange for pay phone (if you don't have a phone in your room)

- [ ] **"C**oming home" clothes and blanket for baby

- [ ] **B**ooks and magazines; paper and pens

- [ ] **B**ox of prunes (for constipation)

- [ ] **S**nacks for partner during labor

- [ ] **B**arrettes, rubber bands, or headband for hair

- [ ] **C**amera and film: Be sure to check the batteries before you pack!

- [ ] **A** bottle of champagne to celebrate!

- [ ] **G**ifts for partner or birthing coach, and/or siblings

Hospital Call List

Name	Relationship	Phone #	Reached
_____	_____	_____	☐
_____	_____	_____	☐
_____	_____	_____	☐
_____	_____	_____	☐
_____	_____	_____	☐
_____	_____	_____	☐
_____	_____	_____	☐
_____	_____	_____	☐
_____	_____	_____	☐
_____	_____	_____	☐
_____	_____	_____	☐
_____	_____	_____	☐
_____	_____	_____	☐
_____	_____	_____	☐
_____	_____	_____	☐
_____	_____	_____	☐
_____	_____	_____	☐
_____	_____	_____	☐
_____	_____	_____	☐

Name	Relationship	Phone #	Reached
_____	_____	_____	☐
_____	_____	_____	☐
_____	_____	_____	☐
_____	_____	_____	☐
_____	_____	_____	☐
_____	_____	_____	☐
_____	_____	_____	☐
_____	_____	_____	☐
_____	_____	_____	☐
_____	_____	_____	☐
_____	_____	_____	☐
_____	_____	_____	☐
_____	_____	_____	☐
_____	_____	_____	☐
_____	_____	_____	☐
_____	_____	_____	☐
_____	_____	_____	☐
_____	_____	_____	☐
_____	_____	_____	☐
_____	_____	_____	☐
_____	_____	_____	☐
_____	_____	_____	☐

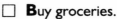

CHECKLIST FOR PARTNER, FRIEND, OR FAMILY MEMBER

☐ **B**uy last-minute baby items. (See Last-Month Checklist, Preparing-the-Nursery Checklist, and Guidelines for Choosing Equipment.)

☐ **B**uy formula. Your pediatrician will tell you which brand and type he/she prefers.

☐ **R**ent a breast pump if needed. Hand pumps are relatively inexpensive and portable. Electric models are more efficient. These can be purchased from large toy stores and pharmacies, rented from pharmacies and medical supply stores, or borrowed from the La Leche League and some hospitals.

☐ **B**uy groceries.

☐ **P**ay bills.

☐ **A**rrange for food/flowers for religious ceremony; arrange for minister/priest to perform ceremony.

☐ **C**hange sheets on Mom and partner's bed.

☐ **D**ouble-check that all medical supplies for Mom have been purchased.

☐ **P**repare baby's bassinet, crib, or temporary bed. Call furniture store to arrange delivery if items have been ordered and have not yet been delivered.

- [ ] **B**uy diapers, cotton balls, creams, and so forth, if not in the house.

- [ ] **A**lert baby nurse of baby's arrival, if you plan to use one.

- [ ] **A**lert diaper service.

- [ ] **B**uy flowers for Mom.

- [ ] **B**uy gift for Mom. Here are some suggestions:

JEWELRY

Coreen Simpson of Cameo Designs makes cameo jewelry featuring contemporary black women on a white background. Available in stores around the country or write to Cameo Designs, 599 West End Avenue, New York, NY 10024.

BOOKS

Black-Eyed Peas for the Soul: Tales to Strengthen the African-American Spirit and Encourage the Heart, by Donna Marie Williams.

Different and Wonderful—Raising Black Children in a Race-Conscious Society, by Darlene Powell Hopson and Derek Hopson.

The Family of Black America, by Michael Cottman and Deborah Willis. A photographic tribute to the black family from 1920 to the present.

Family Pride, by Donna Beasly. Step-by-step instructions for African-Americans to trace family histories.

Having Your Baby, A Guide for African-American Women, by Hilda Hutcherson, M.D., with Margaret Williams.

In Praise of Our Fathers and Our Mothers: A Black Family Treasury, by Wade and Cheryl Hudson.

Mama's Little Baby, The Black Woman's Guide to Pregnancy, Childbirth and Baby's First Year, by Dennis Brown, M.D., and Pamela A. Toussaint.

Mothers, by Wade and Cheryl Hudson. African–American writers and artists celebrate family.

Raising Black Children, by James P. Comer, M.D., and Alvin F. Pouissant, M.D.

Raising the Rainbow Generation: Teaching Your Children to be Successful in a Multicultural Society, by Dr. Derek Hopson and Dr. Darlene Hopson.

Say Amen: The African–American Family's Book of Prayers, by Chestina Mitchell Archibald.

OTHER

Children, babies, or families are often represented in collectibles that can be found with Afrocentric themes, for example: mother and child figurines, picture frames, baby memory books, tiles, and plates.

If you don't have a gift shop that offers these items, That Old Black Magic Gift Gallery, 163 Mamaroneck Avenue, White Plains, NY 10601, 914-328-7212, can make suggestions and mail order gifts to you.

SINGLE MOTHERHOOD

Becoming a parent is a big job—it means enormous changes in your life. Today, more women than ever before are raising children alone. If your child's father will not be involved in your child's life regularly, there are some issues you should consider before baby is born:

■ Choose a friend or relative to be your birthing coach and to attend childbirth classes with you if you take them.

■ Arrange for someone to take you to the hospital when you go into labor. Have a network of several people, if possible, in the event that your first choice can't be reached when you go into labor.

■ If you have other children, make plans in advance to have someone take care of your children when you go into the hospital.

■ Consider child care options before baby is born if you will be going back to work.

■ It is important for children to be around men who play a role in their lives, and this is particularly true if you have a little boy. This role model can be a relative, friend of the family, or someone from an organization like Big Brothers/Big Sisters of America or an athletic coach.

Resources for Single Mothers

Big Brothers/Big Sisters of America
230 North Thirteenth Street
Philadelphia, PA 19107
215-567-7880

National Organization of Single Mothers
Box 68
Midland, NC 28107
704-888-KIDS

National Women's Health Network
514 Tenth Street N.W., Suite 400
Washington, DC 20004
202-347-1140

Parents Without Partners
8807 Colesville Road
Silver Spring, MD 20910
301-588-9354;
899-637-7974

Single Mothers by Choice
Box 7788
FDR Station
New York, NY 10150
212-988-0993

Single Parent Resource Center
1165 Broadway, Room 504
New York, NY 10001
212-213-7974

Single Parenting in the 90's Network
Pilot Publishing
5910 West Brown Deer Road, Suite 269
Milwaukee, WI 53223
414-268-0209

Single Parents Society
527 Cinnaminson Avenue
Palmyra, NJ 08065
609-424-8872

Women on Their Own
Box 1026
Willingboro, NJ 08046
609-871-1499

Part Three

BUYING EQUIPMENT AND CLOTHING

"Your children need your presence more
than your presents."

—Jesse Jackson, "Down with Dope, Up with Hope"

There's so much baby paraphernalia available today that it's sometimes difficult to know which to choose and what's really necessary to have. These lists are designed to provide you with information about the type of equipment and clothing you'll need for baby and to offer guidelines on how to select these items. There are also two travel checklists with all the essentials to have on hand when going out with baby and a special chart on toys for the first year.

Babies Don't Need Brand-New Everything

Deciding how much equipment and clothing to buy can be overwhelming. Here are some tips.

Guidelines for Choosing Equipment

Details the basic equipment you'll need. You certainly don't have to buy all these things before the baby arrives, but the information will help you ask your friends and relatives to give or lend you equipment they are no longer using. Provides information on what to look for when buying a crib, walker, playpen, high chair, and other basic items. Equipment that does not meet government and industry standards can be *dangerous*. The purchasing information in this checklist is very important to ensure your child's safety.

Guidelines for Buying Children's Clothing

Suggests what to look for in fabric, construction, and design—this can increase the durability and longevity of baby's clothes.

Equipment/Clothing Loan Record

Friends and relatives will probably be lending you baby equipment and clothes. Some will want the items returned, and some won't. As time goes on, you won't remember which item came from which person. When you borrow something, list it here immediately, and you'll really appreciate that you did when it's time to return it.

Guidelines for Choosing Diapers

Explains all the options and various types available from cloth to disposables.

Information about Car Seats

Car seats are one of the most important pieces of equipment you can buy to protect your baby. This chart will help you make a decision on which is the best type for your child.

Information about Strollers and Carriages

There are so many different types of strollers and carriages, you can easily choose the wrong kind because you aren't aware of all your options. This information may help you get it right on the first try.

Day Outing Checklist

Includes everything you'll need for a normal day out with baby, whether for a few hours or all day.

Overnight Checklist

Provides a list of the additional items you'll need if you'll be away from home one night or more.

Age-Appropriate Toys

This will give you an idea of the kinds of toys to buy your child. Remember, every child is different in development and preferences.

Babies Don't Need Brand-New Everything

W hen you find out you're pregnant you want to run out and buy all those cute tiny baby outfits. Even baby carriers and cribs look enticing.

But bear in mind it can get very expensive to buy a complete layette and all the equipment you *think* you'll need. There are some very sound reasons for limiting your purchases for baby:

■ Children grow out of clothes so quickly they hardly ever wear them out, so "hand-me-downs" are almost as good as new. You won't get your money's worth out of new baby clothes the way you will out of a new outfit for yourself, which you may wear for years.

■ You'll probably think you need more equipment than you do. You'll be sorry if you buy everything new and then don't use a lot of it. Some babies don't like certain pieces of equipment, such as wind-up baby swings or swaying bassinets.

■ Most baby clothing is unisex with the exception of pink items and dresses and can be borrowed from a child of the opposite sex from yours.

Don't be intimidated into thinking you need to buy every piece of baby equipment available. The amount of equipment (and clothing) you'll need should be determined by your personal comfort level. The only piece of equipment you absolutely must have is a car seat (even if you don't have a car you'll need it to travel in other people's cars).

While some parents prefer to put newborns in a bassinet or even keep baby in the family bed, as baby gets older you'll more than likely want a crib for safety reasons. If you do use strollers, changing tables, high chairs, and so forth, you *must* make certain they have safety straps. Everything else is your choice.

We suggest you accept as much baby clothing and equipment as friends and family members want to lend or give you. There are also a number of other places to find good "slightly used" baby items:

- thrift shops
- resale and consignment shops
- yard and tag sales
- swap meets

Guidelines
for Choosing Equipment

Cribs

- Mattress fits snugly; mattress height can be adjusted as child grows

- As large a distance as possible between the top side of the rail and the mattress so your child can't climb out

- Corner posts are flush with headboard or footboard so child's head or hands can't get stuck

- Corner posts should be less than ⁵/₈ inch in height

- Space between slats is no wider than 2³/₈ inches

- Stable, solid construction

- Locks on the drop side must lock securely every time side is raised and lowered

- Both sides of crib can be lowered

- Lowering mechanism is easy to use

- Plastic teething guards on top rails

- Nonlead paint used on crib

- Check to see if crib converts to junior bed; you may want this feature

Bassinets and Cradles

■ Sturdy bottom

■ Wide, stable base so it is not easily tipped over

■ Can accommodate standard-size bassinet mattress pads and sheets

Bumper Pads

■ Fit around whole crib

■ Tie or snap in place

■ Have at least six straps

■ Surface is washable or has removable washable covers

Baby Gates

■ Mesh gates are safer than accordion style, but make certain the mesh gates have small holes and do not have any sharp edges on mesh area or metal fittings

■ If gates have vertical slats, the slats should be no more than $2^3/8$ inches apart

■ Avoid hinged joints that can pinch, and sharp hardware and small parts that can break off

■ Permanent gates are sturdier than portable ones

High Chairs

■ Wide base for stability

■ If chair has wheels, make sure wheels can lock

■ Sturdy and easy-to-use safety straps

- Tray can be removed with one hand
- Splash-guard rim to prevent plates from falling off
- Easy to wash: plastic trays are easiest to clean, as are plastic or vinyl seats
- Some high chairs are collapsible; check to see if this is easy to do
- Some newer models have adjustable seat heights
- Some high chairs convert to a table and chair

Changing Tables
- Should have safety straps
- Come in standard heights
- Some sit on top of dresser
- Must be easily washable

Playpens
- Mesh netting with a very small weave; $2^3/_8$ inches maximum width of opening
- Easy to open and close; hinges that lock tightly and will not open accidentally
- Bottom pad should extend to edge of playpen and should be sturdy and easy to clean

Toy Chest
- Hinges on lid should have support locks to hold lid in open position

■ Ventilation holes that will not be blocked if chest is put against wall

Front and Back Baby Carriers

Carriers allow you to carry the baby without using your arms. Front carriers have straps that go over your shoulders, and sling carriers generally rest on your hips. Back carriers, generally not intended for use with newborns, resemble knapsacks (including metal frame). Each type uses a different set of muscles. Try it with baby and purchase the carrier that is most comfortable for you. Some carriers to investigate are Sara's Ride, Snugli, Gerry, Lookabout, and the original Baby Sling.

Check for the following:

■ Lightweight, sturdy, machine-washable fabric

■ Padded shoulder straps

■ Match baby's weight and length to manufacturer's weight and length limits

■ Padded covering over metal frame near baby's face

■ Head and neck support for baby

■ Leg openings that won't allow baby to slide out but that will be comfortable

■ Removable bib

■ Storage pouches

■ Easy to get on or off

Pacifiers

- **S**trong enough not to come apart: one-piece construction is best

- **G**uard or shield must be large enough not to fit in baby's throat

- **S**hield must have ventilation holes

- **H**as no ribbon or string attached

- **S**ome are orthodontically correct

- **Y**our baby may prefer one type over another

- **I**f you don't need to use a pacifier you are better off; some babies don't like them

Baby Rockers/Infant Seats

There are two basic types: One is made of molded plastic and has a handle so you can carry baby in it. The other is made of cloth that is stretched across a metal frame and cannot be used as a carrier. The cloth seat is not as versatile as the molded plastic one but some babies prefer its rocking motion.

PLASTIC

▦ Wide, sturdy base

▦ Nonskid feet

▦ Easy-to-use safety belt

▦ Easy-to-hold carrying handle

▦ Angle of back can be adjusted

▦ Optional rocking position

▦ Adequate padding; removable, washable padding

CLOTH

▦ Cloth seat conforms to baby's shape and weight

▦ Sturdy base and washable fabric

▦ Follow manufacturer's age and weight recommendations

Note: Additional variations of infant seats are being produced; look for the same safety features.

Guidelines for Buying Children's Clothing

Design

- Snaps at bottom for ease of diapering
- Adjustments for growth that add life to garment (adjustable shoulder straps, elastic inserts)
- Wide seams
- Undefined waistlines in one-piece garments
- If item is two-piece, look for longer top (won't ride up)
- Tucks, pleats, and yokes to give longer life to the item
- Not difficult to put over child's head, legs, and arms
- Designs that won't trip child
- Elastic waistbands
- Loose-fitting sleeves

Fabrics

- Natural fibers (exception: buy acrylic instead of wool), either firmly woven or closely knit; soft and absorbent
- Machine washable
- No ironing required
- Bright colors for visibility

Sizing

- **G**o by height and weight, not by size or age*

- **R**oom for normal growth—item won't be too small within a very short time (opt for larger over smaller)

- **E**nough room in crotch for child to move around

- **N**eck, waist, and sleeves are not too tight

Infants sizes are three months, six to nine months, twelve months, eighteen months, twenty-four months (sometimes expressed in pounds also). Toddlers are 2T–4T, boys and girls are 4–6X or 4–7.

Equipment/Clothing Loan Record*

Item	From	Condition	To Be Returned: Yes	No
			☐	☐
			☐	☐
			☐	☐
			☐	☐
			☐	☐
			☐	☐
			☐	☐
			☐	☐
			☐	☐
			☐	☐
			☐	☐
			☐	☐
			☐	☐
			☐	☐

*Keep in mind that older cribs, car seats, and other equipment may not fit current federal safety guidelines. Check all borrowed equipment carefully for safety.

			To Be Returned:	
Item	From	Condition	Yes	No
_____	_____	_____	☐	☐
_____	_____	_____	☐	☐
_____	_____	_____	☐	☐
_____	_____	_____	☐	☐
_____	_____	_____	☐	☐
_____	_____	_____	☐	☐
_____	_____	_____	☐	☐
_____	_____	_____	☐	☐
_____	_____	_____	☐	☐
_____	_____	_____	☐	☐
_____	_____	_____	☐	☐
_____	_____	_____	☐	☐
_____	_____	_____	☐	☐
_____	_____	_____	☐	☐
_____	_____	_____	☐	☐
_____	_____	_____	☐	☐
_____	_____	_____	☐	☐
_____	_____	_____	☐	☐
_____	_____	_____	☐	☐

GUIDELINES FOR CHOOSING DIAPERS

Disposable Diapers

▓ Made of paper and special absorbent ingredients, and have a plastic outer cover.

▓ Available in a variety of brands, sizes, absorbencies, and prices.

Read boxes carefully and choose the size that is appropriate for your baby's weight—small, medium, large, or extra-large. Some new diapers are sized according to baby's development—newborn, infant, crawler, and walker.

Larger packages are more economical than the smaller ones. Store brands are less expensive than name brands.

Main brands are Luvs, Huggies, and Pampers. See which brand fits and works best on your baby.

All major brands now have diapers specifically designed for girls or boys. They have extra padding in strategic locations based on anatomical differences.

▓ Some manufacturers produce biodegradable diapers that are also disposable. These are sometimes more expensive.

▓ Disposable diapers may be more conducive to diaper rash because they are made of synthetic materials and do not "breathe."

Cloth Diapers

- **M**ost are made of woven cotton, though some are made of terry cloth and brushed flannel cotton.

- **M**ost come in rectangular shapes that must be folded. Originally diaper pins were used to secure them, but now many diapers (Aware and Boomers) have Velcro attached. There are now some brands that are gathered at the legs.

- **M**ost must be used with rubber pants or diaper covers (usually with Velcro) to hold moisture in. (Bumpkins have a waterproof outer shell, so no diaper covers are necessary.)

- **M**ay be less likely to lead to diaper rash than disposables.

- **E**ven if you use a diaper service, these are less expensive in the long run than disposables.

- **M**ust be changed more frequently unless you double them or buy diaper linings.

Diaper Covers

- **P**lastic pants.

- **D**ecorative cloth pants lined with plastic or cotton, or unlined.

- **Y**ou can use a Velcro- or snap-closed diaper cover to hold regular diapers in place.

- **T**hese covers are available in a variety of prints and designs.

- Come in different sizes based on weight and age.

- Can be washed at home or sent to diaper service.

Training Pants

- Very absorbent underpants, usually with extra padding in the crotch area.

- Are usually terry cloth or cotton.

- Disposable paper ones have recently entered the market. These are like disposable diapers in the shape of pants.

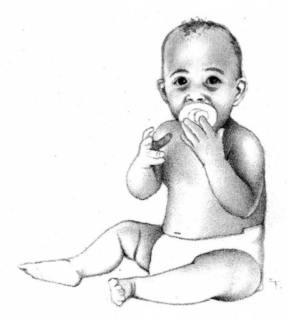

INFORMATION ABOUT CAR SEATS

Do not put your child's car seat in the front seat of the car.

Be sure the car seat you buy has a label on the back that states that the car seat "meets or exceeds federal motor vehicle safety standard 213."

Infant-Only Car Seats

- Designed to be used in rear position only

- Used from birth to twenty pounds (with some exceptions)

- May have a variety of features, including:

  Two- or four-position recline
  Adjustable sun shield
  Removable tray
  Rocker base
  Carrying handles to remove seat and use as baby carrier or to affix to shopping cart
  Cloth or vinyl covers
  Swivel base to allow you to put baby in more easily

Infant/Toddler Car Seats

- Designed to be used in rear position for infants and facing forward for toddlers

- Used from birth to forty pounds (with some exceptions)

■ May have a variety of features, including:

Three- or five-point harness
Several harness positions to adjust as child grows
Several-position growth buckle
Push-button buckle
Adjustable and removable pads
Storage area for toys
Converts to booster seat
Sun shields
Vinyl or fabric covers

Toddler-Only Seats

■ Often called booster seats

■ For use in forward position only for children thirty to sixty pounds (with some exceptions)

■ Vinyl or fabric covers

■ To be used with car seat belts

Accessories

■ Sun shade: attaches to window near baby

■ Car seat cover: terry cloth, easy to remove, machine washable

■ Vinyl seat protector for your car: catches food your baby drops

■ Food tray: attaches to car seat

■ "Doughnut pillow": a roll of fabric that holds infant's head in place

■ Toys that attach to car seat to keep baby amused

INFORMATION ABOUT STROLLERS AND CARRIAGES

Traditional Carriages

- Primarily for infants; stay in one position
- Difficult to store and harder to maneuver
- Sturdier than most strollers
- May be quite expensive
- Lie flat for small baby to sleep in comfort
- Not as useful once baby starts sitting up

Combination Stroller/Carriages

- Available from many manufacturers in a wide variety of models
- Prices range from moderate to quite expensive
- Good for both infant and young child
- Some models convert to a carriage bed
- Handles may reverse for different usages
- Seats and "boot" pads removable for washing
- Four-wheel or two-wheel braking systems
- Accessories include: basket or stroller net, canopy, weather shield, cup holder

Lightweight Strollers

- Available from many manufacturers in a variety of models and price ranges

- Small, lightweight, and collapsible (some can even be folded with one hand, leaving the other free for baby, and others will stand when folded)

- May be lower priced

- Some have adjustable heights for baby's back support (sitting, sleeping, in between)

- Easy to stow in car and carry

Twin Strollers

- May be positioned face-to-face, side-by-side, or one behind the other

- Some can be removed to face in more than one direction

- Check weight and ease of folding

Other Accessories to Be Bought Separately

- Umbrella that attaches to stroller

- Toy bar that goes across the front of the stroller to keep baby amused

- Harness to snap in for very active babies

- Quilted cushion for extra padding

Features to Look for in Any Stroller or Carriage

SAFETY

- Brake locks (rear-locking brake wheels)

- Strong safety belt

- Wide wheel base for stability

- Seat mounted low and deep in the frame

- Backup safety locks to prevent accidental collapse

DURABILITY

- Rustproof

- Unbreakable pieces (nothing that can come off easily)

- Can be used as baby grows bigger

CONVENIENCE

- Easy to use (remember: you'll be loaded down with baby and baby gear)

- Wheels that align well and make steering easy

- Handles that are the right height for you

COMFORT

- Adequate cushioning

- Adequate sun shade

- Adjustable heights for back support

DAY OUTING CHECKLIST

- [ ] **D**iapers (cloth [and diaper covers] or disposable)
- [ ] **P**ortable changing pad
- [ ] **D**iaper cream
- [ ] **B**aby wipes
- [ ] **T**ote bag for dirty diapers
- [ ] **C**otton balls
- [ ] **B**aby lotion, powder, diaper rash medicine
- [ ] **C**hange of clothes
- [ ] **T**owel or diaper for spills
- [ ] **T**oys, rattles, teething toys
- [ ] **S**torybooks
- [ ] **P**acifier (if used)
- [ ] **B**ibs
- [ ] **B**ottles and bottle liners if needed
- [ ] **F**ormula and can opener, juice
- [ ] **C**ookies, crackers, teething biscuits
- [ ] **B**aby food, dish, and spoon

- [ ] **H**airbrush
- [ ] **B**aby carrier
- [ ] **S**troller
- [ ] **I**nfant seat or Sassy Seat (for mealtime)
- [ ] **B**lanket
- [ ] **R**ain poncho
- [ ] **S**un hat
- [ ] **S**unblock

OVERNIGHT CHECKLIST

All items listed for day outings plus:

☐ **P**ortable crib or its equivalent (including sheets and bumpers)

☐ **E**xtra blanket

☐ **N**ight light

☐ **E**xtra diapers

☐ **P**ajamas

☐ **I**tems baby needs to fall asleep (stuffed animal, doll, music box or tape)

☐ **C**lothes, including socks and undershirts

☐ **H**igh chair

☐ **E**xtra bottles

☐ **B**ottle warmer (if used)

☐ **E**xtra baby food and formula

☐ **S**hampoo and baby soap

☐ **D**etergent to wash baby's clothes

☐ **P**lastic bags for dirty diapers and clothes

☐ **C**hildren's acetaminophen (Tylenol or other nonaspirin brand) and thermometer

☐ **C**amera and film

AGE-APPROPRIATE TOYS

*C*aution: **Do not give your child toys with small parts that can fit in his mouth and choke him. Check all toys for sharp edges and loose parts. Follow manufacturer's safety guidelines.**

0–3 Months

Colorful room decorations
Mobiles (black-and-white ones may be easier to see)
Toys strung across crib (use only while baby cannot lift himself)
Soft dolls with clear, distinct facial features
Nonbreakable crib mirror
Music box

3 Months and Older

Soft toys baby can hold
Squeaky toys and rattles
Plastic or rubber teething toys
Gym for crib or playpen
Activity box
Bath toys

6–12 Months

Balls and rolling toys
Stacking toys
Push and pull toys
Pop-up toys
Stuffed animals
Soft cloth books or heavy cardboard books
Soft blocks

Part Four

HEALTH
MAINTENANCE

"Biology is the least of what makes
someone a mother."

—Oprah Winfrey

O f course, one of the most crucial (and anxiety-provoking) aspects of parenthood is taking care of baby's health. This section offers information and organizing tips that will contribute to your baby's well-being.

Pediatrician Interview Form

Will help you evaluate doctors to determine who is best suited to your needs and personality. We suggest choosing a pediatrician before baby arrives and talking to two or three before deciding on the one you'd like to use. Don't be afraid to ask a lot of questions.

First Aid Medical Supply Checklist

All the necessities for routine childhood illnesses and emergency medical care.

Essential Phone Numbers

Includes doctor, fire department, police, baby-sitter . . . the numbers you want to be able to find FAST.

What You Should Know about African-American Children and Asthma

Asthma is becoming more prevalent among black children. Asthmatic children have reactive airways that constrict and make breathing difficult. This information will help you become more knowledgeable about asthma.

Record of Allergies and Reactions

Many children are allergic to foods, medications, insect bites, and so forth. It's important to keep track of these reactions to have an accurate description for your doctor, and so that you can avoid the offending item in the future. Allergic reactions can grow more severe after repeated exposure to the same allergen (such as bee stings and penicillin).

What You Should Know about Sickle-Cell Anemia and African-American Babies

Sickle-cell anemia is most common among African-Americans. While it is a rare disease, here is some basic information you should know.

Special Considerations for African-American Skin and Hair

Contains key facts about bathing, skin, and hair care for your baby.

Infant/Toddler Development Chart

Broad guidelines for when to expect advances or milestones in your child's physical and mental growth; however, please remember *all children are different and develop at their own pace.*

Record of Baby's Height and Weight

Here is something else you may enjoy looking back on. It's also useful if you're concerned about your child's growth in any way.

Baby's Achievements

Gives you a place to record the developments described. You'll appreciate having this information when baby grows up.

Records of Baby's Teeth and Dental Visits

The first few teeth arrive before you know it! Keep a record of these arrivals. Then as baby becomes a toddler, record visits to the dentist and procedures done.

Schedule of Immunizations and Reactions

Although your pediatrician will notify you when your child is due for immunizations, it's useful to be aware of when they are given. This chart will also tell you what type of reactions might occur and how to treat them.

Record of Immunizations

This is an extremely important record to keep. It is imperative that babies and toddlers receive all the appropriate immunizations. In addition, you'll need this information when your child starts school and even at points during his or her adult life.

Medical/Dental Insurance Record

New babies make many visits to the doctor. It's very easy to lose track of when bills are submitted to, or reimbursed by, your insurance carrier if you don't keep an accurate record. In this case, being organized means money in your pocket!

When to Let Your Infant/Toddler Return to Day Care or Play Group

Offers some criteria for deciding when to keep your child home. This can be a tough call for a new parent.

Pediatrician
Interview Form

1. How long have you been in practice? _____
   _____

2. Where did you attend medical school? _____
   _____

3. Where did you do your pediatric residency? _____
   _____

4. Are you board-certified by the American Academy of
   Pediatrics? _____
   _____

5. Do you have a subspecialty? What is it? _____
   _____

6. Did you do any other residencies? _____
   _____

7. Did you do a fellowship? _____
   _____

8. Do you have partners? _____
   _____

9. What are their credentials? _____
   _____

10. How much rotating is there? Will I always see you for
    visits? _____
    _____

11. Who covers for you when you are on vacation? _____
_____

12. What hospital(s) are you affiliated with? _____
_____
_____

13. What are your office hours? Do they include weekends?
_____

14. Are you available at night for emergencies? _____
_____

15. How often do you like to see new babies? _____
_____

16. What are your views on breast-feeding vs. bottle-feeding? _____
_____

17. Will you visit the baby in the hospital after birth? _____
_____

18. Do you have a special time to call for advice? _____
_____

19. What are your fees? _____
_____

20. What insurance plans are you affiliated with? _____
_____

21. Do you have children? _____
_____

Tip: Interview pediatricians *before* baby is born.

First Aid
Medical Supply Checklist

- [ ] **P**etroleum jelly
- [ ] **D**iaper rash cream
- [ ] **A**nti-sting, anti-itch lotion
- [ ] **T**hermometer*
- [ ] **S**afety scissors
- [ ] **A**lcohol
- [ ] **S**terile gauze
- [ ] **L**arge gauze pads
- [ ] **C**oldpack
- [ ] **H**umidifier/vaporizer
- [ ] **F**irst aid chart
- [ ] **E**mergency phone numbers
- [ ] **M**edicine spoon or dropper
- [ ] **S**yrup of ipecac (poison antidote)†

- [ ] **T**ylenol/nonaspirin pain reliever
- [ ] **A**ntibacterial cream
- [ ] **T**weezers
- [ ] **S**terile cotton balls
- [ ] **B**ottle of Pedialyte or other electrolyte solution‡
- [ ] **A**dhesive tape
- [ ] **B**ox of assorted size Band-Aids
- [ ] **E**ar syringe
- [ ] **S**unblock
- [ ] **C**PR chart
- [ ] **B**aby wipes (non-alcohol containing**)
- [ ] **B**aby OraJel for teething

*Fever strip, which is placed on child's forehead, or pacifier that changes color to indicate whether baby has a fever, may also be useful.

†Watch expiration date.

‡Replaces electrolytes lost when child vomits or has diarrhea; Gatorade can also be used. Watch expiration date.

**Will cause less irritation to baby's skin.

ESSENTIAL PHONE NUMBERS

Mother at work _____

Father at work _____

Pediatrician _____
                        (name)   (number)

Hospital _____

Poison control center _____

Police/Emergency _____

Fire department _____

Dentist _____
                        (name)   (number)

Baby-sitter _____
                        (name)   (number)

Day care center _____
                        (name)   (number)

Grandparents _____
                        (name)   (number)

Grandparents _____
                        (name)   (number)

Other relative _____
                        (name)   (number)

Other relative _____
                        (name)   (number)

Neighbor _____
                        (name)   (number)

Neighbor _____
                        (name)   (number)

Friend _____
                        (name)   (number)

Friend _____
                        (name)   (number)

What You Should Know About African-American Children and Asthma

▦ Studies are beginning to show that asthma is more prevalent among African-American children. This condition causes breathing to become difficult owing to tightening of airway muscles. The reason some people have this reaction is unknown.

▦ Common symptoms of asthma include shortness of breath, coughing, and wheezing.

▦ Doctors believe that certain children have airways that tend to overreact to stimuli.

▦ Children of parents with asthma or allergies are more likely to have asthma.

▦ Boys are more likely to have asthma than girls.

▦ Children living in cities are more prone to asthma due to pollutants.

▦ Breast-feeding may lessen the chances of your child's developing asthma.

▦ Keeping your child away from secondhand smoke will also help, as will keeping your home free of allergens such as dust mites, furry animals, cockroaches, and molds.

- **N**early one-third of asthmatic children show signs of the disease by age two. Some outgrow it later in life.

- **D**octors can prescribe medicines to prevent asthma attacks and control them when they occur.

- **S**ome children have exercise-induced asthma.

- **If your child is having difficulty breathing call your doctor immediately.**

Resources for information on asthma:

Allergy and Asthma Network/Mothers of Asthmatics, Inc.
800-878-4403

American Academy of Allergy, Asthma, and Immunology
800-822-ASMA

American Lung Association
800-LUNG-USA

Asthma and Allergy Foundation of America
800-222-LUNG

This mail order catalog offers special products to reduce allergens and dust mites in your home:

National Allergy Supply, Inc.
4400 Abbott's Bridge Road
Duluth, GA 30096
800-522-1448

RECORD OF ALLERGIES AND REACTIONS

U se this form to record any known allergies and possible reactions your child has experienced.

Food	Reaction	Medication/ Treatment	Date
___	___	___	___
___	___	___	___
___	___	___	___
___	___	___	___

Medication	Reaction	Medication/ Treatment	Date
___	___	___	___
___	___	___	___
___	___	___	___
___	___	___	___

Other	Reaction	Medication/ Treatment	Date
___	___	___	___
___	___	___	___
___	___	___	___

Common allergies in young children:

- Food: eggs, strawberries, milk, tomatoes, shellfish, orange juice, nuts, wheat, corn, chocolate. (Please see Part Five, Feeding, for information about lactose intolerance.)
- Medications: antibiotics, including penicillin and sulfa
- Other: insect bites, detergents, wool, scented baby products, pollens, dust, mold

WHAT YOU SHOULD KNOW ABOUT SICKLE-CELL ANEMIA AND AFRICAN-AMERICAN BABIES

■ Within the first few days of life, your baby should be tested for sickle-cell anemia. Sickle-cell anemia is a genetically transmitted disease marked by crescent-shaped red blood cells and is most common among the African-American population.

■ Approximately 8 percent of African-Americans are carriers of the trait, but only about 1 percent actually have the disease.

■ If your child has this chronic disease, he/she will have to be monitored closely by a physician.

■ Sickle-cell can show itself through various medical crises such as:

> Failure to thrive
>
> Swelling, tenderness, and redness of the bones of the hands and feet
>
> Urinary problems
>
> Anemia

Circulatory problems

Infections

■ Your doctor may prescribe penicillin as a preventive measure against these crises.

■ There have been some recent advances in treating sickle-cell disease. Ask your doctor about them.

For further information contact:

Sickle Cell Disease Association of America, Inc.
200 Corporate Pointe, Suite 495
Culver City, CA 90230
800-421-8453

Sickle Cell Disease Branch
Division of Blood Diseases and Resources
National Heart, Lung, and Blood Institute
7550 Wisconsin Avenue, Room 504
Bethesda, MD 20892
301-496-6931
This is a division of the National Institutes of Health.

SPECIAL CONSIDERATIONS FOR AFRICAN-AMERICAN SKIN AND HAIR

Baby's Bath

■ Never leave your baby in the bathtub unattended.

■ Use a mild fragrance-free soap and lukewarm water for your baby's bath. Avoid bubble baths and liquid soaps as they can be irritating to the vaginal area (and can cause urinary tract infections) and to the skin in general.

Baby's Hair

■ Use a specially formulated "no-tears" baby shampoo (with built-in conditioner, if necessary) and tepid water once or twice a week to shampoo your baby's hair.

■ Use your fingers to gently smooth the knots out.

■ You can use a little mineral oil on the scalp if you wish, and a fine comb to gently scrape off cradle cap (the crusty skin on baby's scalp).

■ If you want to braid your baby's hair be sure to use loose braids to avoid breaking the hair. Do not use rubber bands or heavy decorative baubles and beads. If a bead falls off, the baby could swallow it and choke. Be sure to rotate the position of the braids every few days.

Never use hair care products that are not specifically formulated for babies. Chemical relaxers and straighteners
are not meant for babies' hair.

Hot combs and curling irons are safety hazards that can
cause severe burns and are not appropriate for a very
young child's delicate hair.

Baby's Skin

African-American skin tends to be dry. If your baby has
dry skin and you want to put lotion or oil on it, be sure
the product was specifically designed for use on babies. It
should be fragrance-free.

African-Americans are prone to keloids, raised scars. Be
aware that any injury to the skin, including ear-piercing,
may result in a keloid scar. Consult your doctor if you
have any concerns.

Avoid using wipes formulated with alcohol when changing baby's diaper. If you use warm water on cotton balls,
it will be less irritating to baby's skin.

Infant/Toddler Development Chart

The following is only a guideline. If your child does any or all of these things later than this chart suggests, it does not mean there is anything wrong with your child. Likewise, your child is not necessarily exceptional if he or she reaches these stages earlier. All children are different.

Begins to hold head upright
while lying on stomach ..... Six weeks to three months

Notices his/her own hand ..... Six weeks to three months

Smiles .... Six weeks to four months

Laughs .... Two to four months

Turns self over .... Two to five months

Reaches for toy .... Three to four months

Begins whole food .... Six months (depending on
your pediatrician's recom-
mendation)

Begins cow milk .... Six months (depending on
your pediatrician's recom-
mendation)

Cuts teeth .... Three to eighteen months

Sits unsupported .... Five to seven months

Crawls .... Five to eight months

Pulls self up to stand .... Five to ten months

Says "da da" .... Six to eight months

Stands without holding on ... Seven to twelve months

Climbs up stairs .... Seven to ten months

Walks .... Eight to fourteen months

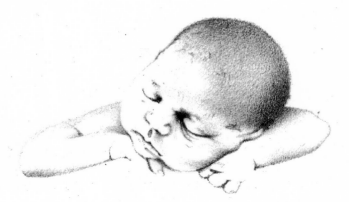

RECORD OF BABY'S HEIGHT AND WEIGHT

	Height	Weight
One-month checkup	_____	_____
Two-month checkup	_____	_____
Three-month checkup	_____	_____
Four-month checkup	_____	_____
Five-month checkup	_____	_____
Six-month checkup	_____	_____
Seven-month checkup	_____	_____
Eight-month checkup	_____	_____
Nine-month checkup	_____	_____
Ten-month checkup	_____	_____
Eleven-month checkup	_____	_____
Twelve-month checkup	_____	_____
Eighteen-month checkup	_____	_____
Twenty-four-month checkup	_____	_____

BABY'S ACHIEVEMENTS

Achievement	Age/Date
First slept through the night	
First turned over	
First smile	
First laugh	
First played with a toy	
First pulled self up	
First sat alone	
First solid food	
First drank from a cup	
First crawled	
First step	
First walked across room	
First ice cream	
First cake	
First fed self	
First word	
First song	
First haircut	

RECORD OF BABY'S TEETH

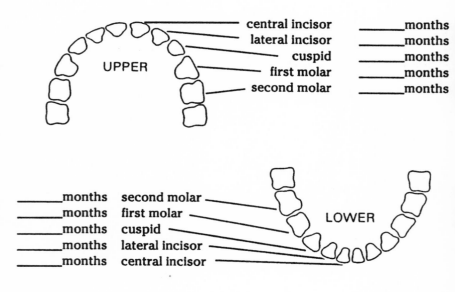

UPPER

central incisor _____months
lateral incisor _____months
cuspid _____months
first molar _____months
second molar _____months

_____months second molar
_____months first molar
_____months cuspid
_____months lateral incisor
_____months central incisor

LOWER

Remember:

- Never put a baby to bed with a bottle of juice or milk. This promotes cavities.
- Teething hurts—use frozen teething rings or a teething gel on baby's gums to ease the pain. Also Baby OraJel.
- Take your child to the dentist for a first checkup between the ages of two and three.
- Brush your child's teeth after every meal. Rub infant's gums with soft cloth or sterile gauze to clean.

RECORD OF DENTAL VISITS

Dentist's Name _____ Phone# _____

Address _____

Date	Checkup	Cleaning	X rays	Fillings	Other

Note: Children should begin seeing the dentist as soon as they have a full set of teeth.

SCHEDULE OF IMMUNIZATIONS AND REACTIONS

Immunization	Timing	Reactions/Treatment
HBV (Hepatitis B)	birth	mild fever
DPT*: diphtheria, pertussis (whooping cough), and tetanus	2 months	soreness at site, mild fever, irritability: treat with cold compresses, fever-reducing, pain-relieving medication
HBV	2 months	mild fever
Oral polio	2 months	no reaction
HIB (H. influenza Type B) for bacterial infections such as meningitis and pneumonia	2 months 4 months	soreness at site, mild fever: give fever-reducing, pain-relieving medication
DPT	4 months	soreness at site, mild fever
Oral polio	4 months	no reaction
DPT	6 months	mild reaction
HIB	6 months	soreness at site, fever
Oral polio	6 months	optional dosage at doctor's discretion
HBV	6 months	mild fever

*In rare cases, children can have a problem with this vaccine. If your child has any history of convulsions, the doctor should be told beforehand. If your child runs a very high fever in reaction to a shot, or cries inconsolably for several hours, call your doctor.

Immunization	Timing	Reactions/Treatment
Tuberculin test	9 months/ additional at doctor's discretion	redness and mild swelling at site if positive; otherwise no reaction
Rubella (German measles), measles, mumps	15 months	mild rash, some fever: give pain-relieving, fever-reducing medication
DPT	15 months	mild reaction
Oral polio	15 months	no reaction
HIB	15 months	soreness at site, fever
DPT	4 to 5 years	mild reaction
Oral polio	4 to 5 years	no reaction
Rubella, measles, mumps	5 years (optional)	mild rash, some fever 7 to 10 days after shot
Tetanus and diphtheria (adult)	14 to 16 years	mild reaction

Note: timing of immunizations may vary slightly in accordance with individual state laws. If a child has a cold or other medical problems, immunizations may be delayed until child is well. Any unusual reactions should be reported to your pediatrician. You may want to do some reading about immunizations before your child receives them.

RECORD OF IMMUNIZATIONS

	Date	*Booster Date(s)*
DPT	_____	_____
Measles	_____	_____
Mumps	_____	_____
Polio	_____	_____
HIB	_____	_____
HBV	_____	_____
Rubella	_____	_____
Other	_____	_____
	_____	_____
Tuberculin test	_____	_____
Blood type	_____	_____
Cholesterol test	_____	_____

Notes: _____

_____

_____

MEDICAL/DENTAL INSURANCE RECORD

Date	Doctor	Reason

Date Submitted	Insurance Company	Date Paid

Date Submitted	Insurance Company	Date Paid
_____	_____	_____
_____	_____	_____
_____	_____	_____
_____	_____	_____

Date	Doctor	Reason
_____	_____	_____
_____	_____	_____
_____	_____	_____
_____	_____	_____
_____	_____	_____
_____	_____	_____
_____	_____	_____
_____	_____	_____
_____	_____	_____
_____	_____	_____

Date Submitted	Insurance Company	Date Paid
_____	_____	_____
_____	_____	_____
_____	_____	_____
_____	_____	_____

When to Let Your Infant/ Toddler Return to Day Care or Play Group

I f your child has been sick and not attending his/her day-care arrangement, when can he/she return? Here are some guidelines*:

1. Temperature of 100 degrees or more (orally or rectally)—child should have normal temperature for twenty-four hours before returning.
2. Sore throat or swollen glands—child should remain at home until pediatrician says it's okay to return.
3. Red eyes or discharge from eyes—child should remain at home until pediatrician says it's okay to return.
4. Croupy, hacking, or persistent cough—child should remain home until cough subsides.
5. Diarrhea or vomiting—child should remain home until well for twenty-four hours.
6. Sores or rash on body or face—child should remain home until cleared by pediatrician.
7. Yellow or green nasal discharge—child should remain home until symptom clears.

Note: These guidelines apply to toddlers and older children. When infants are ill, check with your pediatrician.

*These guidelines are courtesy of Stephen Boris, M.D., F.A.A.P., Mamaroneck, New York.

Part Five

FEEDING

"I want to leave my children and grandchildren
with a mentality that says, 'I can fight to get a
piece of the American Pie.' "

—Dorothy Brunson, American broadcasting
executive

Feeding a new baby is always of great concern to parents, who wonder when to feed, how much to feed, when to start solid food, when to start giving cow's milk, and so on. We won't try to tell you when to do these things because these decisions should be made with the help of your pediatrician. What we will do in this section is provide you with useful charts for recording all those important aspects of feeding your baby—and yourself.

Feeding Tracking Forms

If you're bottle-feeding, you'll want to keep track of how much milk baby is taking and how often. If you're breast-feeding, you'll want to note how often baby is nursing and for how long. It will help you to begin establishing a schedule and may be useful information for your pediatrician if baby is not gaining enough weight.

Food Introduction Record

It is highly recommended that you give baby only one new food every five days in order to determine which food may trigger an allergic reaction. After a few weeks it can be hard to remember which foods were introduced when. This form will serve as a reminder.

Lactose Intolerance in Children

Some children have difficulty digesting milk products. Here's what you should know about lactose intolerance.

Information about Formula

Formula comes in many different varieties. We've provided you with a chart to show all types available. You can decide which formula is best for you.

Information about Baby Bottles and Nipples

Here's some basic information you'll need when selecting these items.

Mother's Exercise Record

Try a little exercise to shed those extra pounds more quickly and strengthen those stomach muscles. Every little bit helps—even if you can only do a few minutes at a time, write it down and see how the minutes add up.

Homemade Baby Food; Baby Food Recipes

Although commercial baby foods are greatly improved these days (less salt, sugar, and preservatives), many new parents still prefer to make their own baby food. If you find some good recipes, here's the place to store them.

Children and Ethnic Foods

Share ethnic foods with your children. We've provided a list of cookbooks for you.

Grocery List

When you have to buy so many items for baby in addition to your regular groceries, you almost always forget something. These lists are foolproof—take them with you whenever you go shopping.

Bottle-Feeding Tracking Form

I f you are bottle-feeding, fill in the time feeding began and the total number of ounces consumed. Your new baby will probably need to be fed approximately every four hours. Keep these records until you feel comfortable that your baby is drinking enough and gaining weight.

MONDAY

Time Started ___ ___ ___ ___ ___ ___ ___ ___ ___ ___

Amount (ounces) ___ ___ ___ ___ ___ ___ ___ ___ ___ ___

TUESDAY

Time Started ___ ___ ___ ___ ___ ___ ___ ___ ___ ___

Amount (ounces) ___ ___ ___ ___ ___ ___ ___ ___ ___ ___

WEDNESDAY

Time Started ___ ___ ___ ___ ___ ___ ___ ___ ___ ___

Amount (ounces) ___ ___ ___ ___ ___ ___ ___ ___ ___ ___

THURSDAY

Time Started   __ __ __ __ __ __ __ __ __ __

Amount (ounces) __ __ __ __ __ __ __ __ __ __

FRIDAY

Time Started   __ __ __ __ __ __ __ __ __ __

Amount (ounces) __ __ __ __ __ __ __ __ __ __

SATURDAY

Time Started   __ __ __ __ __ __ __ __ __ __

Amount (ounces) __ __ __ __ __ __ __ __ __ __

SUNDAY

Time Started   __ __ __ __ __ __ __ __ __ __

Amount (ounces) __ __ __ __ __ __ __ __ __ __

BREAST-FEEDING TRACKING FORM

I f you are breast-feeding, fill in the time nursing began and ended. Remember to alternate breasts and note which breast you ended with so that you begin with the same one next time. Your new baby will probably need to be fed more often than every four hours since it is difficult to determine how much milk the baby's receiving. Keep these records until you feel comfortable that your baby is drinking enough and gaining weight.

MONDAY

Time started

Time ended

Breast ended with (L or R)

TUESDAY

Time started

Time ended

Breast ended with (L or R)

WEDNESDAY

Time started

Time ended

Breast ended with (L or R)

THURSDAY

Time started   __ __ __ __ __ __ __ __

Time ended   __ __ __ __ __ __ __ __

Breast ended with (L or R) __ __ __ __ __ __ __ __

FRIDAY

Time started   __ __ __ __ __ __ __ __

Time ended   __ __ __ __ __ __ __ __

Breast ended with (L or R) __ __ __ __ __ __ __ __

SATURDAY

Time started   __ __ __ __ __ __ __ __

Time ended   __ __ __ __ __ __ __ __

Breast ended with (L or R) __ __ __ __ __ __ __ __

SUNDAY

Time started   __ __ __ __ __ __ __ __

Time ended   __ __ __ __ __ __ __ __

Breast ended with (L or R) __ __ __ __ __ __ __ __

FOOD INTRODUCTION RECORD

The first solid food babies are usually given is rice cereal. Then they are gradually introduced to other cereals. Next, most pediatricians recommend fruits, followed by vegetables and meats. Be sure to heed your doctor's suggestions. Some babies are allergic to or cannot tolerate certain foods, so it is a good idea to introduce one new food at a time and to wait five days before trying another new food.

Foods that most often cause allergic reactions are: nuts, shellfish, chocolate, wheat, orange juice, berries, tomatoes, eggs, milk, and corn.

Do not give your baby honey for the first year and a half because it may contain tiny amounts of botulism which may be too much for an infant's delicate digestive system.

Food	Amount	Date	Reactions

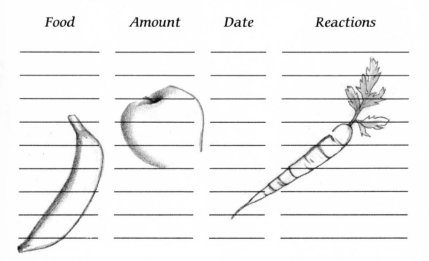

Food	Amount	Date	Reactions

LACTOSE INTOLERANCE IN CHILDREN

Lactose intolerance is a type of digestive disorder in which a child's body is unable to break down milk sugar, or lactose, into forms the body can use. This is caused by a shortage of the enzyme lactase. After the age of two, children's bodies begin to decrease production of lactase. This problem is far more common in people with African, Asian, or Jewish ancestry.

The symptoms of lactose intolerance include nausea, cramps, bloating, gas, and diarrhea within 30 to 120 minutes after eating foods containing lactose (dairy products).

When small, children who are lactose-intolerant should not have any foods containing lactose. Older children probably won't have to avoid lactose entirely, but the amount they can tolerate is individual. It takes trial and error to learn the acceptable quantity.

Lactose intolerance is not dangerous, but children need calcium in their growing years to develop strong bones. If a child cannot drink milk, the calcium needs to come from other sources. Good sources include vegetables like broccoli, Chinese cabbage, collard greens, kale, and turnip greens. Other good sources are soy, tofu, and salmon.

For adults, and possibly older children, there are pills with lactase additives that can be taken with dairy products and there is lactose-reduced milk.

If you suspect lactose intolerance in your baby or young child, contact your doctor immediately. Babies may be put on soy formula, but only your doctor can make that decision.

Here are some resources to learn more about lactose intolerance:

American Academy of Allergy & Immunology
611 East Wells Street
Milwaukee, WI 53202
414-272-6071

American Allergy Association
Box 7273
Menlo Park, CA 94026
415-322-1663

Food Allergy Network
10400 Eaton Place, Suite 107
Fairfax, VA 22030
703-691-3179

National Institute of Allergies and Infectious Diseases
9000 Rockville Pike
Building 31, Room 7A32
Bethesda, MD 20892
301-496-5217

INFORMATION ABOUT FORMULA

Ask your pediatrician what brand of formula you should give your baby. Most formulas are milk-based. Babies with allergies or digestive problems may fare better with soy-based or other formulas.

Most prepared formulas come in the following forms:

1. Ready-to-use (no dilution necessary)
   - 32-ounce can
   - 8-ounce can
   - Disposable bottles: 4 ounces, 6 ounces, and 8 ounces

2. Concentrated (must be diluted with water)
   - 13-ounce can

3. Powdered (must be mixed with water)
   - 16-ounce can

4. Soy formulas
   - For babies who have trouble digesting regular formula. (Your doctor will tell you if your baby needs this type.)

5. "Advanced" formulas
   - Intended for use by older babies. By the time most babies would need this formula, they are usually ready for cow's milk.

Ready-to-use formulas are more expensive but more convenient. If you decide to use the concentrated or powdered forms, be sure to follow diluting and mixing instructions carefully so baby gets the right amount of nutrients.

Tips on storage: Formula in original bottles and cans does not need to be refrigerated. If you open a can and divide it into individual bottles, you must refrigerate the bottles. If you don't use all of it in 24 hours, then throw it out. Some people prefer not to prepare all the bottles at one time. You may simply cover the open can with aluminum foil and store it in the refrigerator. Mark the can with the date and time opened so you know to discard it after 24 hours.

Tips on storage of breast milk: Breast milk may be stored in the refrigerator for 24 to 48 hours. Breast milk may also be frozen for short amounts of time. Purchase special bottles for this purpose or sterile plastic containers, since glass might crack.

INFORMATION ABOUT BABY BOTTLES AND NIPPLES

G lass, plastic, and disposable bottles are available in 4-ounce (for the younger infant) and 8-ounce sizes. All can be covered with caps to protect from spillage and dirt.

Glass Bottles

- Heavy to hold.
- May break or chip if dropped.
- Very durable if you plan to sterilize your bottles (see section on cleaning below).

Plastic Bottles

- Light in weight and easy to hold.
- Available in clear plastic as well as opaque colors; may be decorated with pretty designs.
- Different manufacturers produce bottles in various shapes. Some are easier for baby to hold, such as those with indentations or a hole in the middle, or handles that allow baby's fingers to grip the bottle. Traditional (round) bottles, however, are easier to clean than the more unusually shaped ones.

Disposable Bottles

- Consist of a hard plastic holder in which a soft plastic bottle-shaped bag is inserted. As baby drinks, the bag deflates. This results in less air in the bottle and less air for baby to swallow. After feeding, the plastic bag insert is discarded.

- Eliminates bottle washing.
- More expensive than other bottles.
- Possibility of leakage, if bag is not inserted properly.

Nipples

- Traditionally made of rubber latex, though silicone nipples have recently been developed. Some bottle manufacturers recommend specific nipples for their bottles.
- Come in a variety of shapes. Some are round, some are square, and some try to replicate a mother's nipple shape. Your child may prefer one shape over another.
- For premature or small infants whose sucking ability is weak, softer nipples are available.
- There are nipples that work best with formula, milk, juice, or water. Each has a different hole or opening to allow optimal flow of liquid. The manufacturer's packaging clearly notes which kind of nipple you are buying.

Cleaning Bottles

Many doctors no longer feel sterilizing of bottles is necessary. Check with your pediatrician. Washing with warm, soapy water may be sufficient. Electric and stove-top sterilizers are available, as are special dishwasher racks to hold bottles and nipples. If you cannot find them in a store, contact your dishwasher manufacturer. Nipple brushes and bottle brushes are a must for washing by hand.

Bottle Warmers

Warming the formula is not necessary, but some babies prefer it warm. Electric models are now available. Never heat a baby bottle in a microwave oven.

MOTHER'S EXERCISE RECORD

Try to do a little bit of exercise every day. Even if it's just a few minutes at a time. You'll feel better physically and emotionally and regain your shape faster. (See mail–order section for exercise videos.) Unfortunate information: A zns-tudy in *Obesity Research* shows that heavyset black women burn fewer calories when at rest than white women.

Date	Type of Exercise	Duration (Minutes)

Date	Type of Exercise	Duration (Minutes)

HOMEMADE BABY FOOD

S ome mothers prefer to make their own baby food rather than purchase the bottled variety. It is not difficult, but you do need a food processor or a food grinder to make the food the right consistency.

To make sure that your child gets the right amount of nutrition from the food you make, we recommend that you consult some recipe books for ideas. Here are some suggestions:

The Baby Cookbook, by Karen Knight and Jeannie Lumley
Baby Food Cookbooks & Recipe References: An Index, by the Cookbook Consortium Information Division Staff, ed.
The Complete New Guide to Preparing Baby Foods, by Sue Castle
Feed Me! I'm Yours, by Vicki Lansky
Instant Baby Food, by Linda McDonald
Into the Mouths of Babes: A Natural Foods Cookbook for Infants & Toddlers, by Susan Firkaly
The Natural Baby Food Cookbook, by Margaret Elizabeth Kenda and Phyllis S. Williams
The Vegetarian Mother Baby Book, by Rose Elliot

Handy tip: Make batches of food and freeze in ice trays. Thaw one cube at a time to make one serving for baby.

BABY FOOD RECIPES

Name of Dish _____ Yield _____
Ingredients:
Directions:

_____

Name of Dish _____ Yield _____
Ingredients:
Directions:

_____

Name of Dish _____ Yield _____
Ingredients:
Directions:

_____

Name of Dish _____ Yield _____
Ingredients:
Directions:

_____

CHILDREN AND ETHNIC FOODS

O nce our children are old enough to eat table food (around one year), they are ready to try any foods that are traditional in our families. Feeding our children foods that come out of the African–American experience is an important way for them to learn about our heritage.

Spicy foods won't hurt young children, but they, like adults, don't need an excess of fat or salt. Introduce new foods one at a time (to watch for allergies). Be cautious with "gassy" vegetables like beans and peas, which can cause stomach distress.

The following is a brief listing of some of the cookbooks available:

The African Cookbook, Bea Sander (Citadel Press, $13.95)

The African–American Heritage Cookbook, Carolyn Quick Tilbert (Birch Lane Press, $13.95)

The Black Family Reunion Cookbook: Recipes and Food Memories, National Council of Negro Women (A Fireside Book/ Simon and Schuster, $12.00)

Dori Sanders Country Cooking, Dori Sanders (Algonquin Books of Chapel Hill, $18.95)

Ideas for Entertaining from the African–American Kitchen, Angela Shelf Medearis (Dutton, $27.95)

Kwaanza, Eric V. Copage (Quill, $18.95)

Mother Africa's Table, National Council of Negro Women (Main Street Books, $18.95)

Soul Food: Recipes and Reflections from African-American Churches, Joyce White

A Taste of Heritage—The New African-American Cuisine, Joe Randall and Toni Tipton-Martin

A special note: Some African-Americans have traditionally given their babies "gripe water" to calm a colicky baby or for an upset stomach. This homemade remedy contains alcohol, which can be harmful to your baby and is not recommended!

Grocery List

- ☐ **F**ormula
- ☐ **C**otton balls
- ☐ **B**aby shampoo
- ☐ **D**iapers
- ☐ **A**&D ointment/Vaseline
- ☐ **S**unscreen
- ☐ **T**eething toys
- ☐ **P**edialyte
- ☐ **B**aby wipes

- ☐ **B**ottle liners
- ☐ **B**aby soap
- ☐ **B**aby powder
- ☐ **Q**-tips
- ☐ **B**aby Tylenol
- ☐ **T**eething gel
- ☐ **P**rescriptions
- ☐ **D**isposable bibs
- ☐ **D**iaper liners

Household toiletries:

_____

_____

_____

_____

Baby Food—Cereal

_____

_____

_____

_____

Baby Food—Vegetables

_____

_____

_____

_____

Baby Food—Cookies

_____
_____
_____
_____

Baby Food—Fruit/Juice

_____
_____
_____
_____

Baby Food—Meat

_____
_____
_____
_____

Miscellaneous

_____
_____
_____
_____

Cleaning Products

_____
_____
_____
_____

Dairy

_____
_____
_____
_____

Canned Goods

_____
_____
_____
_____

Paper Goods

_____
_____
_____
_____

Meat/Poultry/Fish

_____

_____

_____

_____

Fruit/Vegetables

_____

_____

_____

_____

Snacks/Desserts

_____

_____

_____

_____

Bread/Crackers

_____

_____

_____

_____

Pasta/Rice/Grains

_____

_____

_____

_____

Condiments

_____

_____

_____

_____

Frozen Foods

_____

_____

_____

_____

Beverages

_____

_____

_____

_____

Part Six

Selecting and Evaluating Child Care

"I can make something out of (the) children . . .
They have the essence of greatness in them."

—Zora Neale Hurston, *Moses, Man of the Mountain*

$\mathcal{C}$ hoosing a caregiver or a day-care center for your child can be a very emotional issue. You'll feel better about it if you are prepared and practical about deciding who to entrust with the care of your child. The interview/evaluation forms we've included in this section are for four different situations.

Adult Caregiver Interview Form

The types of questions you will want to ask someone who regularly takes care of your child will differ somewhat from those asked of an occasional baby-sitter. Please add your own questions to the interview form.

Day Care or Preschool Evaluation Form

Another tough decision. There are big differences among day care centers; again, use our form as a guide and add your own questions.

Interview Form for Choosing Home-Based Child Care

Another option for child care that should be carefully researched. Use this checklist to get a complete picture.

Child Care Resources

A list of organizations that can provide information about how to get good child care.

Teenage Baby-sitter Interview Form

A little shorter than the previous form. While you are concerned for your child's welfare, you are not making a decision about whether someone can nurture your child on an ongoing basis. But you do want someone trustworthy, reliable, and mature enough to handle an emergency. Here are some questions to determine that.

Baby-sitter Instruction Street

Allows you to leave all the information you need in one convenient place.

Baby-sitter Directory

Provides a handy place to keep a list of baby-sitters and relevant information about them.

ADULT CAREGIVER INTERVIEW FORM

Applicant's name _____

Address _____

Phone number _____

1. What experience do you have with caring for children?

   _____

2. What was your last job? _____

   How long were you there? _____

3. If child care, what were your exact duties? Please
   describe what you did on a typical day. _____

   _____

4. Can you provide references? _____

   _____

   _____

5. What do you think your former employer will say
   about you? _____

   _____

6. Why are you no longer working there? _____

   _____

7. Have you ever been convicted of any crime? _____

8. Would you allow me to do a background check on you?

   _____

9. If previous job was not child care, why have you decided
   to work in child care? _____

10. Have you ever taken a baby-sitter or child CPR course?

_____

   Where was it given? _____

   When? _____

11. What was the level of school you attended? _____

12. Do you smoke? _____

13. Do you have any health problems? _____

14. Are you a U.S. citizen or do you have a green card? _____

_____

15. Do you have a driver's license? _____

   Car? _____

16. Can you stay late if I have to work late or go out of
   town? _____

_____

17. Where do you live? _____

   Can you get here by _____ A.M. so that I can get to work
   on time? _____

18. Describe all aspects of job and discuss these with the
   applicant. Be certain to stress your philosophy and those
   things that are most important to you, including:
   ■ Hours of duty
   ■ Job requirements—feeding, bathing, taking child for
     walks, taking child to play with other children
   ■ Household responsibilities—laundry, cleaning,
     cooking

19. Be specific about how much you wish the caregiver to be
   a part of the family. For example, will she eat meals with
   the family, spend leisure time with the family, etc.?

20. If caregiver is to be live-in:
   - Show her the bedroom and bathroom she would use
   - Be specific about what hours she is expected to be on duty
   - Establish whether she goes home on weekends or lives with you seven days a week
   - Discuss days off
   - Explain how you feel about her entertaining friends

21. Discuss salary and any benefits you might provide, including paid vacations.

22. Add your own questions here: _Do You have any experience with premature babies?_

Questions to ask yourself after the interview: _____

1. Does the applicant appear warm and friendly? _____

2. How did she interact with my child? _____

3. Was she easy to talk to? _____

4. Did she seem willing to follow instructions? _____

Other impressions:

DAY CARE CENTER OR PRESCHOOL EVALUATION FORM

Name of center or school _____

Address _____

Telephone _____

1. What are the hours the center/school is open? _____

2. How many children are in the center/school? _____
   How many children per room? _____
   What are their ages? _____
   What is the staff/child ratio? _____

3. What are the qualifications and credentials of the director and staff? _____
   _____
   _____

4. What is the philosophy of the school or center? _____
   _____

5. Is there any parent participation? _____

6. How are parents notified when there is a problem? _____
   _____

7. Is there a religious affiliation? _____

8. What kind of license or accreditation does the center/school have? _____
   _____

9. How long has the center/school been in business? _____

10. What is the cost? _____

_____

Does it increase as the child gets older? _____

11. Is transportation available? _____
    What does it cost? _____

12. Describe a typical day. _____

_____

_____

_____

13. Do children go outside during the day? _____

14. What is the policy for sick children? _____

15. Is formula, juice, or snack provided? _____

16. Will center/school follow your basic rules for your
    child? _____

17. How much staff turnover is there? _____

18. What kind of insurance does the center have? _____

19. Is there a nap time? _____

20. Are there any provisions for children who need to come
    earlier or stay later than regular hours? _____
    What does this cost? _____

Visit Center/School and Note the Following:

1. Size and appearance of indoor *and* outdoor facilities

_____

_____

2. General atmosphere _____

_____

_____

_____

_____

3. Do children look happy? _____

4. Are children busy? _____

5. Is the staff interested and involved? _____

6. How are the children disciplined? _____

_____

7. Is there a rest/nap area? _____

8. Is there an eating area? Is it clean? _____

9. How clean are the entire facility, toys, equipment, and so forth? _____

10. Are there enough toys/activities? _____

11. Are there sick children present? _____

12. Is there a comfortable transition from one activity to another? _____

_____

13. Do the children have their own cubbyholes? _____

_____

_____

14. Are there any "enhancement" programs such as an early childhood music or art curriculum? _____

_____

_____

Interview Form for Choosing Home-Based Child Care

An alternative to a day care center or preschool is family day care. This is a situation in which several children are cared for in a family setting. The following are questions to ask this kind of child care provider:

1. How long have you been providing home child care services? _____

2. Do you have any other related experience? _____
_____

3. How many children do you care for? _____
_____

4. What are the ages of the children that you care for?
_____

5. What hours will you keep my child? _____
_____

6. Do you have any children of your own? _____
_____

7. Do you smoke? _____
_____

8. How is your health? _____

_____

9. Are you licensed? _____

10. Are you the owner of this house? _____

11. What kind of insurance do you have? _____

_____

12. Have you ever been convicted of a crime? _____

_____

13. Do the children go outside? _____
    Do you stay outside with them? _____

_____

14. Do you have outdoor play equipment? _____

_____

15. Is your yard fenced in? _____

16. Do you have toys? _____ Videos? _____
    Riding vehicles? _____

17. Do you have any dogs or cats? _____

18. Do any of your neighbors have dogs? _____

19. What is your daily schedule? _____

_____

20. What rooms do the children play in? _____

_____

21. When do you feed the children? _____

_____

22. Do you have any help? _____

_____

23. Do you have any backup if you're sick? _____

    _____

24. Do you keep firearms in your home? _____

    _____

25. Do you have safety latches on the cabinets and toilets
    and windows? Do you have gates near the stairways? Do
    you have electrical socket covers? _____

    _____

26. How far is the nearest fire station? _____

    _____

    Fire hydrant? _____

    What is your escape route in case of fire? _____

    _____

27. Do you have smoke detectors? _____
    Carbon monoxide detectors? _____
    A burglar alarm? _____

28. Have you taken any child care classes? _____
    CPR classes? _____

29. What do you do if one child is sick? _____

    _____

30. Do you require proof that children have immuniza-
    tions? _____

31. What would you do if my child swallowed poison?

    _____

32. What would you do if my child passed out? _____

    _____

33. What would you do if my child was bleeding badly?

    _____

34. What would you do if my child stopped breathing?

    _____

35. Where do you keep emergency phone numbers? _____

    _____

36. How do you handle toilet training? _____

    _____

37. Do you charge by the day, week, month? _____

    _____

38. What are the holidays on which you don't provide child
    care? _____

    _____

CHILD CARE RESOURCES

Child Care Action Campaign
330 Seventh Avenue, 17th Floor
New York, NY 10001
212-239-0138
National advocacy organization to increase and improve child care services. Has a bimonthly newsletter and free information guides.

Child Care Aware
2116 Campus Drive S.E.
Rochester, MN 55904
800-424-2246
This national initiative was designed to improve the quality and availability of child care. Offers publications, toll-free hotline, and referrals.

National Association for Family Child Care
725 Fifteenth Street N.W., Suite 505
Washington, DC 20005
202-347-3300
This association promotes high standards for all day care operations. Runs an accreditation program and gives referrals.

Resources for Parents, Teachers, Caregivers
Resource Center
Cornell University
1 Cornell Business & Technology Park
Ithaca, NY 14850
Offers a free brochure listing booklets, fact sheets, videotapes, and guides that are available.

Software

SAE Software
670 South Fourth Street
Edwardsville, KS 66113
800-530-5607;
913-441-1868
Free demo available, first aid basics: "Safety First: A Guide to Safe Child Care for Baby-sitters" (DOS).

TEENAGE BABY-SITTER
INTERVIEW FORM

Applicant's name _____ Phone number _____

Address _____

1. How old are you? _____

2. Do you have any brothers or sisters? _____

3. Can you give references? _____

   _____

4. Have you ever baby-sat before? _____

5. Have you ever baby-sat an infant before? _____

6. Have you ever fed an infant? _____

7. Have you ever changed an infant's diapers? _____

8. Have you ever taken a baby-sitter course or a child CPR
   course? _____

   When and where was it given? _____

9. Which days/nights are you available? _____

   _____

10. Do you smoke? _____

11. Do you have any health problems? _____

12. What is your hourly charge? _____

13. Will you need us to pick you up and/or drive you
    home? _____

    _____

14. Why do you want to baby-sit? _____

15. You might want to make up a situation to determine how it would be handled, such as: If my two-year-old son swallowed kitchen cleanser, what would you do?

_____

16. Discuss rules and policies about having friends over, using the phone, smoking or drinking, and so forth.

Impressions: _____

_____

_____

_____

_____

BABY-SITTER INSTRUCTION SHEET

Our name _____

Address _____
_____

Our phone number _____

Child(ren) name(s) _____
and age(s) _____

We are at: _____
Name/address _____
_____

Phone number _____

Emergency Phone Numbers

Police _____ Fire _____

Ambulance _____ Poison center _____

Neighbor _____

Relative _____

Instructions for Today

Meals and snacks _____

Don't give these foods to my baby: popcorn, nuts, hot dogs, grapes

Medications _____

☐ Change diaper every _____ hours

☐ Change diaper before bed

☐ Give bath

TV instructions _____

Other instructions _____

IMPORTANT
Never leave child alone
Take child out of house if fire is suspected
Call fire department from next door
Don't open the door for anyone

PARENTS REMEMBER TO:
Show baby-sitter how doors and locks open
Show locations of exits
Show locations of alarms or smoke detectors

Baby-Sitter Directory

Name _____ Phone _____ Age _____
Address _____
_____
Times available _____
Hourly wage _____ Needs transportation _____
Comments _____
_____

Name _____ Phone _____ Age _____
Address _____
_____
Times available _____
Hourly wage _____ Needs transportation _____
Comments _____
_____

Name _____ Phone _____ Age _____
Address _____
_____
Times available _____

Hourly wage _____ Needs transportation _____

Comments _____

_____

Name _____ Phone _____ Age _____

Address _____

_____

Times available _____

Hourly wage _____ Needs transportation _____

Comments _____

_____

Name _____ Phone _____ Age _____

Address _____

_____

Times available _____

Hourly wage _____ Needs transportation _____

Comments _____

_____

Name _____ Phone _____ Age _____

Address _____

_____

Times available _____

Hourly wage _____ Needs transportation _____

Comments _____

_____

Part Seven

BUYING BY MAIL ORDER

"A child is a quicksilver fountain
spilling over with tomorrows and tomorrows
and that is why
she is richer than you or I."

—Tom Bradley, *The Impossible Dream*

There are many, many places to shop for children's products today—no doubt your friends will have some great recommendations for you. But if your time for shopping is limited, and you don't want to carry heavy packages while you're pregnant or busy with baby, we'd like to suggest that you consider mail order.

There are literally hundreds of mail-order companies selling the following: maternity clothes, children's clothing, equipment and furniture, toys, books, records, tapes, linens, birth announcements, and many other items useful for babies. Included in this section you will find:

Tips for Buying by Mail Order

If you haven't done much ordering by mail, these suggestions may be helpful to you.

Mail Order Purchasing Record

Here's the place to keep a record of items ordered.

Mail Order Resources

This is by no means a complete list of all mail-order companies offering child-related products. However, most of the better-known ones are represented here, and there should be enough choices to allow you to purchase almost anything you might need by mail. Companies are listed by the type of product they sell.

TIPS FOR BUYING
BY MAIL ORDER

1. Always keep track of what you have ordered, when you ordered, and your method of payment.
2. Use 800 numbers, credit cards, and faxing to speed your order.
3. Never send cash.
4. Read size information carefully. If you're still not sure, call the company or catalog and ask about how sizes run.
5. Don't be afraid to return. Always save all packing materials until you are sure you will not be returning anything.
6. Don't be afraid to use the customer service number most mail order companies provide if you want to check on your order or a return.
7. Remember colors may not look exactly the same as they appear in the catalog.
8. Allow three to six weeks for delivery of your order.
9. Credits take two billing cycles to appear on your credit card statement, so don't panic if you don't see them right away.
10. If you have trouble with a mail order company, contact the Federal Trade Commission, the post office, your state attorney general's office, and/or the Direct Marketing Association (6 East Forty-third Street, New York, NY 10017) for help.
11. By law, if a mail order company cannot ship to you in thirty days of receipt of your order (unless otherwise stated in their offer), the company must give you the option of receiving a refund or waiting for the order to be filled.

MAIL ORDER
PURCHASING RECORD

Company/catalog ordered from (include address and phone)

_____

_____

Items ordered:

_____

_____

_____

Date ordered _____ Method of payment _____

Received ☐   Returned ☐   Date _____   Refund received ☐

Company/catalog ordered from (include address and phone)

_____

_____

Items ordered:

_____

_____

_____

Date ordered _____ Method of payment _____

Received ☐   Returned ☐   Date _____   Refund received ☐

Company/catalog ordered from (include address and phone)

_____

_____

Items ordered:

_____

_____

_____

Date ordered _____ Method of payment _____

Received ☐   Returned ☐   Date _____   Refund received ☐

Company/catalog ordered from (include address and phone)

_____

_____

Items ordered:

_____

_____

_____

Date ordered _____ Method of payment _____

Received ☐   Returned ☐   Date _____   Refund received ☐

Company/catalog ordered from (include address and phone)

_____

_____

Items ordered:

_____

_____

_____

Date ordered _____ Method of payment _____

Received ☐   Returned ☐   Date _____   Refund received ☐

Company/catalog ordered from (include address and phone)

_____

_____

Items ordered:

_____

_____

_____

Date ordered _____ Method of payment _____

Received ☐   Returned ☐   Date _____   Refund received ☐

Company/catalog ordered from (include address and phone)

_____

_____

Items ordered:

_____

_____

_____

Date ordered _____ Method of payment _____

Received ☐   Returned ☐   Date _____   Refund received ☐

Company/catalog ordered from (include address and phone)

_____

_____

Items ordered:

_____

_____

_____

Date ordered _____ Method of payment _____

Received ☐   Returned ☐   Date _____   Refund received ☐

MAIL ORDER RESOURCES

Baby Announcements

A Star is Born
6462 Montgomery Avenue
Van Nuys, CA 91406
818-785-5656
Looks like the slates used to start the "take" of a movie.

Babygram
201 Main Street, Suite 600
Fort Worth, TX 76102
800-345-BABY
Looks like a real Mailgram, with your message and baby's photo.
Can obtain envelopes to address in advance.

Baby Name-A-Grams
Box 8465
Saint Louis, MO 63132
314-966-BABY
Baby's name is drawn in calligraphy to become a design such as a
sheep or a bear.

Birthwrites
Box 684
Owings Mill, MD 21117
301-363-0872
Offers a wide variety.

Cradlegram
Box 16-4135
Miami, FL 33116
305-595-6050
Printed on pink or blue paper; name and vital statistics put into
rhyming message.

H & F Products
3734 West Ninety-fifth Street
Leawood, KS 66206
800-338-4001
Many designs with matching thank-you notes. Envelopes available
in advance.

Heart Thoughts, Inc.
6200 East Central, Suite 100
Wichita, KS 67208
316-688-5781
Formal, with baby's own calling card. Can be ordered in advance
and card inserted when baby is born.

Send, Inc.
800-752-SEND
Carries African-American-oriented announcements. Hallmark
Cards now has "Mahogany," an African-American division.

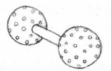

Baby Equipment

Baby & Company
Box 906
New Monmouth, NJ 07748
908-671-7777
Supplies for infants and toddlers.

Baby Bunz & Co.
Box 1717
Sebastopol, CA 95473
707-829-5347
Sells cloth diapers and diaper covers.

Baby's Comfort Products
1740 North Old Pueblo Drive
Tucson, AZ 87545
602-624-1892
Car seat covers and other useful items.

Best Selection, Inc.
2626 Live Oak Highway
Yuba City, CA 95991
916-673-9798
Useful baby equipment and safety items.

Birth And Beginnings
6828 Route 128
Laytonsville Shopping Center
Laytonsville, MD 20879
301-990-7925
Diaper covers, training pants, and other items.

Chaselle, Inc.
9645 Gerwig Lane
Columbia, MD 21046
800-CHASELLE;
800-492-7840 in Maryland
Baby supplies that are also sold to day care centers.

The Children's Warehouse
1110 Technology Place, Suite 108
West Palm Beach, FL 33407
(no phone orders)
Basic baby equipment from name-brand manufacturers. Some
items at sale prices.

Compare And Save Premium Catalog
Box 88828
Seattle, WA 98188
800-COMPARE
Discounted baby merchandise from diapers to high chairs.

Designer Diapers
3800 Wendell Drive, Suite 403
Atlanta, GA 30336
800-541-7604;
404-691-4403
Disposable diapers. Expensive but cute gift items.

Good Gear For Little People
Washington, ME 04574
207-845-2211
Good selection of carriers, outerwear, and other items for children at reasonable prices.

Hand-in-Hand
9180 Le Saint Drive
Fairfield, OH 45014
800-543-4343
Lots of useful equipment for infants and toddlers.

Heir Affair
625 Russell Drive
Meridien, MS 39301
800-332-4347;
601-484-4323
Baby equipment and toys.

Mother's Network
875 Avenue of the Americas
Suite 2001
New York, NY 10001
212-239-0510
Excellent catalog full of useful items.

One Step Ahead
Box 46
Deerfield, IL 60015
800-274-8440
Nice selection of baby and toddler supplies.

Perfectly Safe
7425 Whipple Avenue N.W.
North Canton, OH 44720
216-494-4366
Safety and other useful items for infants, toddlers, small children, moderately priced.

The Right Start Catalog
Right Start Plaza
5334 Sterling Center Drive
Westlake Village, CA 91361
800-LITTLE 1
Safety and other useful items for infants, toddlers, and small children.

Selfcare Catalog
Box 130
Mandeville, LA 70470
800-345-3371
Health and safety items for babies and children.

Sensational Beginnings
Box 2009
430 North Monroe
Monroe, MI 48161
800-444-2147;
313-242-2147
Good selection of infant and toddler equipment.

Seventh Generation
Colchester, VT 05446
800-456-1177
Environmentally safe disposable diapers, cloth diaper covers, cotton flannel diapers, chlorine-free baby wipes, "unpetroleum" jelly for baby.

The following manufacturers will send you catalogs but do not sell by mail order:

Aprica Kassai USA, Inc.
Box 25408
Anaheim, CA 92825
800-444-3312;
714-634-0402
Will send catalog on strollers.

Century Products, Inc.
9600 Valley View Road
Macedonia, OH 44056
216-468-2000
Will send literature on their strollers and other baby equipment.

Graco Children's Products, Inc.
Route 23
Elverson, PA 19520
800-345-4109;
215-286-5921
Will send literature on strollers and other baby equipment.

Perego U.S.A., Inc.
3625 Independent Drive
Ft. Wayne, IN 46818
219-482-8191
Will send literature on their strollers.

Children's Clothing

After The Stork
1501 Twelfth Street N.W.
Albuquerque, NM 87104
505-243-9100
Complete line of cotton clothing for infants, toddlers, and older children.

At Last, Inc.
Building 32
Endicott Street
Norwood, MA 02062
(no phone orders)
Clothes for children with sizing problems. Sizes 4 to 14.

Baby Clothes Wholesale
70 Ethel Road West
Piscataway, NJ 08854
908-842-2900
Discounted infant and young children's clothing.

Biobottoms
Box 6009
Petaluma, CA 94953
707-778-7945
Cotton clothing and diaper covers.

Bright's Creek
Bay Point Place
Hampton, VA 23653
800-622-9202;
804-827-1850
Full line of infants, toddlers, and children's clothing.

Children's Shop
Box 625
Chatham, MA 02633
800-426-8716
High-quality clothing for babies and children.

Children's Wear Digest
Box 22728
2515 East Forty-third Street
Chattanooga, TN 37422
800-433-1895
Clothing and linens for infants, toddlers, and older children.

Chock Catalog Corp.
74 Orchard Street
New York, NY 10002
800-222-0020
Brand-name underwear, sleepwear, and socks for infants, children, and adults.

Classics For Kids
10501 Metropolitan Avenue
Kensington, MD 20895
301-949-3128
Natural-fiber clothing for infants and children.

Garnet Hill
262 Main Street
Franconia, NH 03580
800-622-6216
Complete line of infants' and children's clothes and linens. All made of natural fibers.

Hanna Andersson
1010 Northwest Flanders Street
Portland, OR 97209
800-222-0544
All-cotton clothing from Sweden. Infants, children, and mothers.

Karin And John
525 South Raymond Avenue
Pasadena, CA 91105
800-626-9600
Cotton infants' and children's clothing from Sweden.

Lands' End Kids Catalog
1 Lands' End Lane
Dodgeville, WI 53595
800-356-4444
Good-quality clothing from the people who make Lands' End adult clothing.

Maggie Moore
Box 1564
New York, NY 10023
212-543-3434
High-quality clothing for infants and children.

Olsen's Mill
Highway 21
Box 2266
Oshkosh, WI 54903
414-685-6688
Oshkosh B'Gosh clothing for infants, children, and adults.

Patagonia Functional Kids Clothes
1609 West Babcock Street
Box 8900
Bozeman, MT 59715
800-638-6464
All the great Patagonia outdoor wear in kids' sizes.

Petit Pizzazz
2134 Espey Court No. 10
Crofton, MD 21114
301-858-1221
Clothing for babies and children. Made in the United States and Sweden.

Richman Cotton Company
529 Fifth Street
Santa Rosa, CA 95401
800-992-8924
All-cotton clothing for babies, children, and adults.

Simplicity Pattern Co.
2 Park Avenue
New York, NY 10016
888-588-2700
A catalog is available for maternity, infant, and toddler clothes and decorating patterns.

Storybook Heirlooms
1215 O'Brien Drive
Menlo Park, CA 94025
800-899-7666
Unusual dresses for girls, and some special items like rocking chairs.

The Wooden Soldier
North Hampshire Common
North Conway, NH 03860
603-356-7041
Unusual, charming outfits for infants, toddlers, older children—sailor suits, velvet dresses, sleepwear, and so forth.

Children's Furniture

Boston and Winthrop
2 East Ninety-third Street
New York, NY 10128
212-410-6388
Hand-painted children's furniture.

Furniture Designs
1827 Elmdale Avenue
Glenview, IL 60025
708-657-7526
Furniture plans for the do-it-yourselfer. High chairs, cribs, and so
forth.

JCPenney Baby and You Catalog
Catalog Distribution Center
11800 West Burleigh Street
Box 2021
Milwaukee, WI 53201
800-222-6161
Wide selection of baby furniture and equipment.

Laura D's Folk Art Furniture, Inc.
106 Gleneida Avenue
Carmel, NY 10512
914-228-1440
Hand-painted folk art furniture that is functional.

Squiggles and Dots
Box 870
Seminole, OK 74868
405-382-0588
Very lovely, unusual pieces.

Tabor Industries
8220 West Thirtieth Court
Hialeah, FL 33016
305-557-1481
Cribs, changing tables, rocking chairs, and so forth.

Children's Music and Videotapes

CHILDREN'S MUSIC AND VIDEOTAPES WITH AFRICAN-AMERICAN CONTENT

African-American Video Library
California Newsreel
149 Ninth Street
San Francisco, CA 94103

Audio Forum
Suite M7
96 Broad Street
Guilford, CT 06437
203-453-9794
Music of Africa, music for Kwanzaa.

"Grins, Giggles, Coos" video;
Infantology
Box 567144
Atlanta, GA 33156
770-730-9267
Features African-American babies.

Schoolmaster Videos
745 State Circle
Box 1941
Ann Arbor, MI 48106
800-521-2832
Series of tapes about African-Americans including Medgar Evars, Jackie Robinson, A Woman Called Moses.

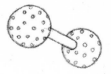

CHILDREN'S MUSIC AND VIDEOTAPES (GENERAL)

Alcazar Records
Box 429
Waterbury, VT 05676
800-541-9904
Distributes independent labels—has special children's catalog.

Audio Therapy Innovations
Box 550
Colorado Springs, CO 80901
800-537-7748
Has books but also useful tapes to lull infants to sleep.

Children's Book and Music Center
2500 Santa Monica Boulevard
Santa Monica, CA 90404
800-443-1856;
213-829-0215
Large catalog of books, records, tapes, videos, and musical instruments.

Educational Activities
Box 87
1937 Grand Avenue
Baldwin, NY 11510
800-645-3739;
516-223-4666
Records, audio and videocassettes.

Educational Record Center
1575 Northside Drive
Atlanta, GA 30318
800-438-1637
Records, tapes, and videos, from infants to teens.

A Gentle Wind
Box 3103
Albany, NY 12203
518-436-0391
Children's musical cassettes.

Kimbo Educational
Box 477
Long Branch, NJ 07740
800-631-2187;
908-229-4949
Nursery rhymes, educational aids, on records and cassettes.

Linden Tree
170 State Street
Los Altos, CA 94022
414-949-3390
Records and cassettes of children's favorites.

Music for Little People
Box 1460
Redway, CA 95560
800-346-4445
Records and cassettes by popular children's artists.

Parentcare Ltd.
6 Commercial Street
Hicksville, NY 11801
800-334-3889
Wide variety of children's videos.

Playskool Lullabies
Hasbro Direct
Box 6147
Waterville, OH 43081
(no phone orders)
Audiocassettes personalized with your child's name.

San Francisco Music Box Company
Box 7817
San Francisco, CA 94120
800-227-2190;
415-653-3022
Large selection of music boxes.

Sweet Baby Dreams
200-F Del Vina Avenue
Monterey, CA 93940
408-659-3259
Lullabies and music to promote sleep.

Vid America
Box 5240
FDR Station
New York, NY 10150
(no phone orders)
Children's videocassettes.

Gifts for Expectant Families

Daddy's Tees
Box 160214
Miami, FL 33116
800–541–7202;
305–271–2073
Gift T–shirts for new fathers and grandparents.

The Right Start Catalog
Right Start Plaza
5334 Sterling Center Drive
Westlake Village, CA 91361
800–LITTLE 1
Gifts for grandparents and siblings.

Children's Linen

Cloud Nine
142 Loma Alta
Oceanside, CA 92054
619-722-1676
Futons, sheets, comforters.

Company Store
500 Company Store Road
LaCrosse, WI 54601
800-356-9367
Down comforters, bumper pads.

Cuddledown
42 North Elm Street
Box 667
Yarmouth, ME 04096
800-323-6793;
207-846-9781
Comforters and flannel sheets.

Domestications
Hanover, PA 17333
717-633-3333
Inexpensive sheets, quilts, and towels for children.

Moncour's
4233 Spring Street, Suite 14
La Mesa, CA 92041
800-541-0900
Crib sheets, comforters, bumpers, quilts, etc.

Pine Creek Company
28000 South Dryland Road
Canby, OR 97013
503-266-7463
Flannel crib sheets, bumper pads, comforters, and so forth, and some cotton baby clothing as well.

Rue de France
78 Thames Street
Newport, RI 02840
800-777-0998
Lace curtains.

Children's Books

CHILDREN'S BOOKS WITH AFRICAN-AMERICAN CONTENT

Children's Small Press Collection
719 North Fourth Avenue
Ann Arbor, MI 48104
800-221-8056

Claudia's Caravan
Box 1582
Alameda, CA 94501
510-521-7871
Multicultural books, dolls, tapes, games.

Dover Books
31 East Second Street
Mineola, NY 11501
516-294-7000

Great Owl Books
800-299-3181
Multicultural books.

COMICS WITH AFRO-AMERICAN THEMES

Brother Man
Original Man
U.N. Force

PUBLISHERS OF BOOKS FOR AFRICAN-AMERICAN CHILDREN

Albert Whitman and Company
6340 Oakton Street
Morton Grove, IL 60053
847-581-0033

**Bantam Doubleday Dell
Random House, Inc.**
1540 Broadway
New York, NY
212-354-6500

Clarion Books
215 Park Avenue S.
New York, NY 10003
212-420-5800

HarperCollins
10 East Fifty-third Street
New York, NY 10022
212-207-7000

Holiday House
425 Madison Avenue
New York, NY 10017
212-668-0085

Lee & Low Books
95 Madison Avenue
New York, NY 10016
212-779-4400

Little, Brown
34 Beacon Street
Boston, MA 02108
617-227-0730

Penguin Putnam
375 Hudson Street
New York, NY 10014
212-366-2000

Scholastic, Inc.
55 Broadway
New York, NY 10012
212-343-6100

Simon & Schuster
1230 Avenue of the Americas
New York, NY 10020
212-698-7200

Umbrella Press
50 Rivercourt Boulevard
Toronto, Ontario
M4J 3A4 Canada
416-696-6665

Workman Publishing
708 Broadway
New York, NY 10003
212-254-5900
Workman Publishing publishes *Black Heritage Brainquest* for children. You may be interested in looking at the *Quarterly Black Review of Books*—your library may have it.

AFRICAN-AMERICAN BOOKSTORES

Afrocentro Books
333 South State Street
Chicago, IL 60604
312-939-1956

Apple Book Center
7900 West Outer Drive
Detroit, MI 48235
313-255-5221

Black Books Plus
702 Amsterdam Avenue
New York, NY 10025
212-749-9632

Black Images Book Bazaar
230 Winnewood Village
Dallas, TX 75224
214-943-0142

Hue-Man Experience
911 Park Avenue W.
Denver, CO 80205
303-293-2665

Karibu Books
3393 Donelle Drive
Forestville, MD 20747
301-736-6170

Phoenix Book Store
381 North E
San Bernadino, CA 92401
909-383-2329

CHILDREN'S BOOKS (General)

Better Beginnings Catalog
345 North Main Street
West Hartford, CT 06117
800-274-0068;
203-236-4907
Books and tapes for babies and children.

Blacklion Books
9 East Oxford Avenue
Alexandria, VA 22310
(no phone orders)
Books of all kinds for babies and young children.

Chinaberry Book Service
2830 Via Orange Way
Suite B
Spring Valley, CA 92078
800-777-5205;
619-670-5200
Large selection of children's books.

Gryphon House
Early Childhood Catalog
Box 275
Mount Rainier, MD 20712
800-638-0928;
301-779-6200
Good selection of preschool books.

Herron's Books for Children
Box 1389
Oak Ridge, TN 37830
(no phone orders)
Books and puzzles for young children.

Tapes and Cassettes on Parenting

Baby Safety Video
SI Video
Box 3100
San Fernando, CA 91341
(no phone orders)
Complete information about how to make your home baby-safe.

Babyworks
4343 Equity Drive
Box 1667
Columbus, OH 43216
(no phone orders)
Video series on caring for baby.

Feeling Fine Programs
3575 Cahuenga Boulevard N., Suite 440
Los Angeles, CA 90068
213-851-1027
Videos on pregnancy, childbirth, breast-feeding, postnatal exercise.

Los Angeles Birthing Institute
4529 Angeles Crest Highway, Suite 209
La Canada, CA 91011
818-952-6310
Books on childbirth and parenting.

Super Sitters
Box 7020
Brick, NJ 08723
800-722-9999
Set of books and video to educate baby-sitters.

Toys and Educational Items

AFRICAN-AMERICAN AND MULTICULTURAL TOYS

Hand-in-Hand
891 Main Street
Oxford, ME 04270
800-872-9745
Carries multicultural toys.

The Natural Baby Co.
816 Silva Street
800 B-S
Trenton, NJ 08628
609-771-9233

MANUFACTURERS OF BLACK-ORIENTED TOYS

W. B. Adams Puzzles and Games
1551 Valley Forge Road
Lansdale, PA 19446
215-699-7774
Emphasizes black history.

Briarpatch
30 Forest Street
Montclair, NJ 07042
201-744-0936;
800-232-7427
Sells West African activity kit.

Colorful World-Multicultural Toys
10301 Main Street, Suite 306
Fairfax, VA 22003
703-764-2990
Mail order toys for African-American children.

Hasbro
1027 Newport Avenue
Pawtucket, RI 02861
401-727-5800
Makes Tuskegee Airmen dolls.

Mattel
333 Continental Boulevard
El Segundo, CA 90245
213-524-2348
Makes African-American Barbie.

Olmec Corp.
2408 Ownby Lane
Richmond, VA 23220
804-358-7557
Black dolls and action figures. Largest minority-owned toy business in the country.

Rainbow Brite Doll Collection/Up, Up and Away Co.
250 West Fifty-fourth Street
New York, NY 10019
212-245-8484
There are black dolls in the collection.

TOYS AND EDUCATIONAL ITEMS (GENERAL)

Abilities International
Old Forge Road
Elizabethtown, NY 12932
518-873-6456
Developmental toys and educational items.

Back to Basics Toys
3715 Thornapple Street
Chevy Chase, MD 20815
800-356-5360
Many traditional and ultra-modern toys.

Bear-in-Mind
53 Bradford Street
West Concord, MA 01742
508-369-1167
The best in stuffed bears.

Childcraft
20 Kilmer Road
Edison, NJ 08818
800-631-5657
Educational toys and games; infant toys.

Constructive Playthings
1227 East 119th Street
Grandview, MO 64030
816-761-5900
Good selection of infant toys, games, and toys for young children.

Coyote Collection Puzzles
94349 Deadwood Creek Pond
Deadwood, OR 97430
503-964-5621
Lovely educational wooden puzzles and silkscreened wood-framed mirrors for children.

Cuddle Toys
PO Drawer D
Keene, NH 03431
800-992-9002;
603-352-3414
High-quality stuffed animals.

Early Learning Centre
Box 821
Lewiston, ME 04243
800-255-2661
Good selection of infant and preschool toys and games.

FAO Schwarz
Box 182225
Chattanooga, TN 37422
800-426-TOYS
Fabulous toys from the famous New York toy store.

Fisher-Price Bits And Pieces Catalog
Consumer Affairs
636 Girard Avenue
East Aurora, NY 14052
(no phone orders)
Replacement parts for Fisher-Price toys.

Growing Child
Box 620
Lafayette, IN 47902
317-423-2624
Toys for babies and children to age ten.

Hearth Song
Box B
Sebastapol, CA 95473
800-325-2502
Unusual toys and baby items. Many imported.

Just For Kids
Box 29141
Shawnee, KS 66201
800-654-6963
Toys and games for infants, toddlers, and older children.

Learning Materials Workshop
58 Henry Street
Burlington, VT 05401
802-862-8399
Block and construction sets.

Lilly's Kids
Virginia Beach, VA 23479
804-430-1500
Nice line of toys and educational items.

Marvelous Toy Works
2111 Eastern Avenue
Baltimore, MD 21231
301-276-5130
Wooden toys and block sets, well-priced.

Mill Pond Farms
Box 203
Rochester, MA 02770
(no phone orders)
Wooden toys imported from New Zealand.

Playfair Toys
1690 Twenty-eighth Street
Boulder, CO 80301
303-440-7229
Good selection of infant items, toys, and games.

Sesame Street Catalog
2515 East Forty-third Street
Chattanooga, TN 37422
800-446-9415
Toys and products with all the wonderful Sesame Street characters.

Toys to Grow On
2615 East Dominguez Street
Box 17
Long Beach, CA 90801
800-542-8338;
213-603-8890
Nice selection of toys and games.

Walt Disney Kids Catalog
Box 29144
Shawnee Mission, KS 66201
800-237-5751
T-shirts, toys, and stuffed animals with imprints from Mickey and other Disney characters.

Maternity and Nursing Clothes

Beegotten Creations
Box 1800
Spring Valley, NY 10977
800-772-3390
T-shirts and sweatshirts for all members of the expecting family.

Bosom Buddies
Box 6138
Kingston, NY 12401
914-338-2038
Nursing bras.

Decent Exposures
Box 736
2202 Northeast 115th Street
Seattle, WA 98215
206-364-4540
Nursing bras and tummy "slings."

Fifth Avenue Maternity
Box 21826
Seattle, WA 98111
800-426-3569
High-fashion, attractive, and casual clothing, suitable for business. Nightgowns and underwear.

JCPenney Catalog
Catalog Distribution Center
11800 West Burleigh Street
Box 2021
Milwaukee, WI 53201
800-222-6161
A good selection of maternity clothes.

Motherhood
390 Sepulveda Boulevard
El Segundo, CA 90245
800-421-9967;
310-364-1100
Wide range of basic maternity clothes.

Mother's Work
1309 Noble Street
Fifth Floor
Philadelphia, PA 19123
215-625-9259
Conservative clothing for the working woman.

Page Boy
8918 Governor's Row
Dallas, TX 75247
800-225-3103
Upbeat sportswear and business clothing.

Reborn Maternity
564 Columbus Avenue
New York, NY 10024
212-362-6965
Selections from their stores. For work and play; conservative.

Recreations Maternity
Box 091038
Columbus, OH 43209
800-621-2547;
614-236-1109
Selections from their stores; somewhat conservative.

NURSING SUPPLIES

Breastfeeding—The Art of Mothering
Alive Productions Ltd.
Box 72
Port Washington, NY 11050
516-767-9235
Videotape written by a pediatrician.

Lait Ette Co.
183 Florence Avenue
Oakland, CA 94618
415-655-5110
Storage system for chilling and transporting expressed milk.

La Leche League
Box 1209
Franklin Park, IL 60131
312-455-7730
Books, breast pumps, milk storage systems, breast shields.

Lopuco Ltd.
1615 Old Annapolis Road
Woodbine, MD 21797
800-634-7867;
301-489-4949
Hand-operated breast pumps.

Mother Nurture Project
103 Woodland Drive
Pittsburgh, PA 15228
412-344-5940
Everything you need for breast-feeding.

Part Eight

RESOURCES

"I have a dream my four little children will one day live in a nation where they will not be judged by the color of their skin but by the content of their character."

—Martin Luther King Jr., "I Have a Dream" speech given at Lincoln Memorial, Washington D.C., August 28, 1963

Parenting can be an overwhelming experience—especially in the beginning. Don't get discouraged if you feel you don't know the right answers to everything. There are many resources you can call upon for information. This section includes the following:

Organizations

These public and private organizations can provide you with literature and information at little or no cost.

Magazines and Newsletters

A subscription to one of the many publications for parents is a good way to get regular information about parenting.

Useful Information as Your Child Grows

This information pertains to older children but we thought it would be handy to have a list of boarding schools and camps for African-American children and a list of education and historical sites to visit with your children.

Resources on Adoption

This is a list of organizations that can help you in the adoption process.

Parents' Groups and Preschool Activities Record; Child's Friends and Their Parents

You'll find there are a lot of groups in your area run by churches, hospitals, schools, and private organizations. Create your own directory of these, and of your child's friends.

Organizations

ORGANIZATIONS FOR AFRICAN-AMERICAN PARENTS

African-American and Minority Health
Office of Minority Health
Department of Health and Human Services
200 Independence Avenue S.W.
Room 118F
Washington, DC 20201

African National People's Empire Re-Established
13902 Robson Street
Detroit, MI 48227
313-837-0627
Works to promote the health and welfare of African peoples.

Afro-Am Publishing Co.
910 South Michigan Avenue, Suite 556
Chicago, IL 60605
312-922-1147
Compiles data on the African-American experience and has a list
of publications.

Association for the Study of African-American Life and History
1407 Fourteenth Street N.W.
Washington, DC 20005
202-667-2822
Mainly serves college students but offers referrals to younger students interested in African-American culture.

Black Awareness in TV
13217 Livernois
Detroit, MI 48238
313-931-3427

Black Music Association
307 South Broad Street
Philadelphia, PA 19107
215-732-2460
Offers information on black musical heritage through the schools.

Black World Foundation
Box 2869
Oakland, CA 94609
415-547-6633
Information clearinghouse for black culture.

Blacks Educating Blacks about Sexual Health Issues
1528 Walnut Street, Suite 1414
Philadelphia, PA 19102
215-546-4140

Interracial Family Alliance
Box 16248
Houston, TX 77222
713-454-5018

Martin Luther King Jr. Center for Non-violent Studies
449 Auburn Avenue N.E.
Atlanta, GA 30312
404-524-8969

NAACP–Youth and College Division
4805 Mt. Hope Drive
Baltimore, MD 21215
301-358-8900
Teaches kids the realities of the political process.

National Association for Sickle-Cell Diseases
4221 Wilshire Boulevard, Suite 360
Los Angeles, CA 90010
800-421-8453;
213-936-7205

National Black Child Development Institute
1023 Fifteenth Street N.W., Suite 600
Washington, DC 20005
800-556-2232;
202-387-1281
This group does research, lobbies lawmakers, and offers tutoring and mentoring programs. Publishes several newsletters.

National Center for Fair and Open Testing
342 Broadway
Cambridge, MA 02139
617-864-4810

Quality Education for Minorities
1818 N Street N.W., Suite 350
Washington, DC 20036
202-659-1818

Southeastern Regional Office National Scholarship Service and Fund for Negro Students
965 Martin Luther King Jr. Drive
Atlanta, GA 30314
404-577-3990

Sickle Cell Disease Branch
Division of Blood Diseases and Resources
National Heart, Lung and Blood Institute
7550 Wisconsin Avenue, Room 504
Bethesda, MD 20892
301-496-6931
This is a division of the National Institutes of Health.

United Negro College Fund
500 East Sixty-second Street
New York, NY 10021
212-326-1100
Raises general operating funds for forty-one historically black four-year colleges and universities and provides scholarships and loans to 51,000 students.

Visions Foundation
Box 37049
Washington, DC 20013
202-287-3360
Provides educational programs to promote appreciation of black culture in the United States.

ORGANIZATIONS (GENERAL)

American Academy of Pediatrics
Box 927
141 Northwest Point Boulevard
Elk Grove Village, IL 60009
708-228-5005
Has a variety of literature available, including child health record and first aid chart.

American College of Nurse-Midwives
1522 K Street NW, Suite 100
Washington, DC 20005
202-289-0171
Can refer you to a certified nurse-midwife in your area.

American College of Obstetricians and Gynecologists
409 Twelfth Street S.W.
Washington, DC 20024
202-638-5577
Provides educational pamphlets and referral service.

American Dental Association
Department of Public Information
211 East Chicago Avenue
Chicago, IL 60611
312-440-2500
Literature available.

American Mothers, Inc.
The Waldorf-Astoria
301 Park Avenue
New York, NY 10022
212-755-2539
Dedicated to preserving family values. Sponsors local chapters and support networks.

American Optometric Association
243 North Lindbergh Boulevard
St. Louis, MO 63141
314-991-4100
Booklets available: "Your Baby's Eyes" and "Your Preschooler's Eyes."

American Red Cross
National Headquarters
2025 E Street N.W.
Washington, DC 20006
202-728-6475
Local chapters sponsor infant CPR courses and other useful courses. Booklets also available.

ASPO/Lamaze
Box 952
McClean, VA 22101
800-368-4404;
703-524-7802
Organization of childbirth educators who will refer you to local Lamaze instructors.

Childcare Action Campaign
99 Hudson Street, Suite 1233
New York, NY 10013
212-334-9595
A group dedicated to providing a national system of child care. Brochures available.

Children's Defense Fund
122 C Street N.W.
Washington, DC 20001
202-628-8787
Pays attention to the needs of poor, minority, and handicapped children. Publications available.

Child Welfare League of America
440 First Street N.W., Suite 310
Washington, DC 20001
202-638-2952
Children's advocacy group. Books and publications available.

Circumcision Information Center
Box 765
Times Square Station
New York, NY 10108
(phone number not available)
Literature available.

Council for Interracial Books for Children
Box 1263
New York, NY 10023
212-757-5339
Can provide information on choosing nonracist books.

Depression after Delivery
Box 1282
Morrisville, PA 19067
215-295-3994
Will refer you to women who live near you and can help.

Fatherhood Project
Bank Street College of Education
610 West 112th Street
New York, NY 10025
212-663-7200
Provides information on subjects related to fatherhood.

Human Growth Foundation
Box 3090
Falls Church, VA 22043
800-451-6434
Free booklets and growth chart.

International Childbirth Education Association
Box 20048
Minneapolis, MN 55420
612-854-8660
Has an excellent catalog of publications on childbirth, child-rearing, breast-feeding, and circumcision topics.

International Twins Association
c/o Lynn Long and Lori Stewart
6898 Channel Road N.E.
Minneapolis, MN 55432
612-571-3022
Publishes a newsletter.

Juvenile Diabetes Foundation International
432 Park Avenue South
New York, NY 10016
800-223-1138;
212-889-7575
Raises funds for research and has free brochures about pregnancy and diabetes, and babies and diabetes.

La Leche League
Box 1209
9616 Minneapolis Avenue
Franklin Park, IL 60131
708-445-7730
Information and supplies for breast-feeding. Referrals to local chapters.

March of Dimes
1275 Mamaroneck Avenue
White Plains, NY 10605
914-428-7100
Literature on infant care.

National Association of the Deaf
814 Thayer Avenue
Silver Spring, MD 20910
301-587-1788
Catalog of publications, support groups, workshops, seminars, and so forth.

National Association for the Education of Young Children
1834 Connecticut Avenue N.W.
Washington, DC 20009
800-424-2460;
202-232-8777
Dedicated to improving services to young children and families. Books, posters, brochures.

National Association for Family Day Care
815 Fifteenth Street N.W., Suite 928
Washington, DC 20005
202-347-3356
Organiation of day care providers, with membership open to parents. Newsletter, books available.

National Association for Parents of the Visually Impaired
2180 Linway Drive
Beloit, WI 53511
800-562-6265;
608-362-4945
Provides support and information for parents. Several books and resource guides available.

National Center for Learning Disabilities
99 Park Avenue
New York, NY 10016
212-687-7211
Magazine available.

National Coalition Against Domestic Violence
Box 15127
Washington, DC 20003
800-333-7233;
202-293-8860
Twenty-four-hour hot line provides information about shelters and programs. Working to end family violence.

National Committee for the Prevention of Child Abuse
332 South Michigan Avenue, Suite 950
Chicago, IL 60604
312-663-3520
Organization trying to end child abuse. Free catalog of publications.

National Down Syndrome Society
666 Broadway, Suite 810
New York, NY 10012
800-221-4602
Provides information and local references.

National Easter Seal Society
70 East Lake Street
Chicago, IL 60601
312-726-6200
Books and leaflets available, for those with disabilities.

National Federation for the Blind
1800 Johnson Street
Baltimore, MD 21230
301-659-9314
Self-help organization for the blind and visually impaired.

National Institutes of Health
Office of Communications
Editorial Operations Branch
Bethesda, MD 20892
301-496-4000
Free publications list on topics such as childhood hyperactivity, infantile apnea and home monitoring, baby bottle tooth decay, and so forth.

National Organization of Mothers of Twins Clubs
12404 Princess Jeanne N.E.
Albuquerque, NM 87112
505-275-0955
Coordinates local clubs. Will send free informational brochures.

National Sudden Infant Death Syndrome Foundation
10500 Little Patuxent Parkway, Suite 420
Columbia, MD 21044
800-221-SIDS
Provides information and local references.

Parents Anonymous
6733 South Sepulveda, Suite 270
Los Angeles, CA 90045
800-421-0353;
213-410-9732
Network of self-help support groups for parents who are frightened they may hurt their children.

Parents of Prematures
13613 N.E. Twenty-sixth Place
Bellevue, WA 98605
(phone number not available)
Newsletter and other literature available.

Parents of Prematures
c/o Houston Organization for Parent Education, Inc.
3311 Richmond, Suite 330
Houston, TX 77098
(phone number not available)
Has resource directory available.

Parents Without Partners
8807 Colesville Road
Silver Spring, MD 20910
800-638-8078;
301-588-9354
Has nine hundred local chapters and publishes a magazine.

Physicians for Automotive Safety
Box 208
Rye, NY 10580
(phone number not available)
Booklets on car seats.

Single Mothers by Choice
Box 1642
Gracie Square Station
New York, NY 10028
212-988-0993
An association that provides support and information to single
women who are mothers or are considering motherhood.

Magazines and Newsletters

MAGAZINES AND NEWSLETTERS FOR BLACK CHILDREN AND THEIR PARENTS

Black Child
Box 17479
Beverly Hills, CA 90209
213-251-3805
Magazine containing up-to-date information for raising black
children.

Cobblestone
7 School Street
Peterborough, NH 03458
603-924-7209
History for children; some African-American history (ages nine
to fifteen).

The National Black Child Development Institute
1023 Fifteenth Street N.W., Suite 600
Washington, DC 20005
800-556-2234
Publishes *Black Child Advocate* and *Child Health Talk* newsletters.

Skipping Stones
Box 3939
Eugene, OR 97403
541-342-4956
Forum for communication of children around the world (ages
seven to thirteen).

MAGAZINES AND NEWSLETTERS (General)

American Baby
Box 53093
Boulder, CO 80322
800-525-0643
Offers practical advice for parents of infants.

Child Health Alert Newsletter
Box 338
Newton Highlands, MA 02161
(phone number not available)
Reports on latest findings in health-related areas for infants and children.

Child Magazine
Box 3176
Harlan, IA 51593
800-777-0222
Articles on parenting and a strong emphasis on children's fashion.

Exceptional Child Magazine
Parenting Your Disabled Child
605 Commonwealth Avenue
Boston, MA 02215
(phone number not available)
Informative articles for parents of children with disabilities.

Mothering Magazine
Box 1690
Sante Fe, NM 87504
505-984-8116
Articles on parenting approached from a holistic/naturalistic point of view.

Parenting Magazine
501 Second Street
San Francisco, CA 94107
800-525-0643
Useful articles on parenting for those with infants and young children.

Parents Magazine
Box 3055
Harlan, IA 51593
800-727-3682
The original parenting magazine features articles for parents with children of all ages.

Twins Magazine
Box 12045
Overland Park, KS 66212
913-722-1090
This magazine has useful information for parents of twins.

Working Mother
Box 53861
Boulder, CO 80322
800-525-0643
Articles are geared toward working women with families.

Useful Information as Your Child Grows

The following pages include information that pertains to older children, but which we thought would be handy for you to have for future reference.

Traveling with Your Child

As your child gets older, you may be interested in visiting some of the following museums and other historical places of interest:

African Art National Museum
Smithsonian Institution
Washington, D.C.
202-287-3306

Black American West Museum and Heritage Center
Denver, Colorado
303-292-2566

Black History National Recreational Trail
Washington, D.C.
202-619-7222

Boston Black Heritage Trail
Boston, Massachusetts
617-742-5415

California Afro-American Museum
Exposition Park
Los Angeles, California
213-744-0600

Civil Rights Memorial
Montgomery, Alabama
205-427-3317

Delta Blues Museum
Clarksdale, Mississippi
601-624-4461

DuSable Museum of African American History
Washington, D.C.
202-619-7222

King Center
Atlanta, Georgia
404-524-1956

Motown Museum
Detroit, Michigan
312-875-2264

The Museum for African Art
New York, New York
212-966-1313

Schomburg Center for Research in Black Culture
New York, New York
212-491-2207

The Studio Museum in Harlem
New York, New York
212-864-4500

BOARDING SCHOOLS AND CAMPS FOR AFRICAN-AMERICAN CHILDREN

A lthough there were once eighty-three black boarding schools in this country, those listed below represent the schools that have survived. There are over three hundred black private schools in the United States.

Boarding Schools

Laurinburg Institute
125 McGirt Bridge Road
Laurinburg, NC 28352
910-276-0684

Pine Forge Academy
Box 338
Pine Forge, PA 19548
610-326-5800

Piney Woods Country Life School
Box 99
Piney Woods, MS 39148
601-845-7821

Saints Academy and College
Box 419
Lexington, MS 39095
601-834-1019

Southern Normal Academy
Box 408
Brewton, AL 36427
334-867-4831

Summer Camp

Camp Atwater
756 State Street
Springfield, NY 01109
800-245-1110
For kids ages six to fifteen.

RESOURCES ON ADOPTION

Adoptive Families of America
3333 North Highway 100
Minneapolis, MN 55422
612-535-4829
Has 275 adoptive support groups around the world; twenty-four-hour hot line; bimonthly newsletter, mail order catalog.

American Academy of Adoption Attorneys
Box 33053
Washington, DC 20033
(no phone)
Offers state-by-state directory.

American Adoptive Congress
1000 Connecticut Avenue N.W., Suite 9
Washington, DC 20036
202-483-3399
Public information center; referrals, publications, newsletter.

F.A.C.E. (Families Adopting Children Everywhere)
Box 28058
Northwood Station
Baltimore, MD 21239
410-488-2656
Publishes a resource manual and a bimonthly magazine.

Parents' Groups and Preschool Activities Record

Name _____ Location _____
Date/Time _____ Phone# _____

Name _____ Location _____
Date/Time _____ Phone# _____

Name _____ Location _____
Date/Time _____ Phone# _____

Name _____ Location _____
Date/Time _____ Phone# _____

Name _____ Location _____
Date/Time _____ Phone# _____

Name _____ Location _____
Date/Time _____ Phone# _____

Name _____ Location _____
Date/Time _____ Phone# _____

Name _____ Location _____

Date/Time _____ Phone# _____

Name _____ Location _____

Date/Time _____ Phone# _____

Name _____ Location _____

Date/Time _____ Phone# _____

Name _____ Location _____

Date/Time _____ Phone# _____

Name _____ Location _____

Date/Time _____ Phone# _____

Name _____ Location _____

Date/Time _____ Phone# _____

Name _____ Location _____

Date/Time _____ Phone# _____

Name _____ Location _____

Date/Time _____ Phone# _____

Name _____ Location _____

Date/Time _____ Phone# _____

Name _____ Location _____

Date/Time _____ Phone# _____

Name _____ Location _____

Date/Time _____ Phone# _____

Name _____ Location _____

Date/Time _____ Phone# _____

Name _____ Location _____

Date/Time _____ Phone# _____

Name _____ Location _____

Date/Time _____ Phone# _____

Name _____ Location _____

Date/Time _____ Phone# _____

Name _____ Location _____

Date/Time _____ Phone# _____

Name _____ Location _____

Date/Time _____ Phone# _____

Name _____ Location _____

Date/Time _____ Phone# _____

Name _____ Location _____

Date/Time _____ Phone# _____

Name _____ Location _____

Date/Time _____ Phone# _____

Name _____ Location _____

Date/Time _____ Phone# _____

Name _____ Location _____

Date/Time _____ Phone# _____

Name _____ Location _____

Date/Time _____ Phone# _____

Name _____ Location _____

Date/Time _____ Phone# _____

Name _____ Location _____

Date/Time _____ Phone# _____

Name _____ Location _____

Date/Time _____ Phone# _____

Name _____ Location _____

Date/Time _____ Phone# _____

Name _____ Location _____

Date/Time _____ Phone# _____

CHILD'S FRIENDS AND THEIR PARENTS

Before you know it, you'll hear about other babies in your neighborhood, or your child will make friends in a parents' group/day care situation. You may even want to get to know the parents. Here's the place to store those names and numbers.

Child's name _____ Age _____

Parents' names _____ Phone# _____

Address _____

Child's name _____ Age _____

Parents' names _____ Phone# _____

Address _____

Child's name _____ Age _____

Parents' names _____ Phone# _____

Address _____

Child's name _____ Age _____

Parents' names _____ Phone# _____

Address _____

Child's name _____ Age _____

Parents' names _____ Phone# _____

Address _____

Child's name _____ Age _____

Parents' names _____ Phone# _____

Address _____

Child's name _____ Age _____

Parents' names _____ Phone# _____

Address _____

Child's name _____ Age _____

Parents' names _____ Phone# _____

Address _____

Child's name _____ Age _____

Parents' names _____ Phone# _____

Address _____

Child's name _____ Age _____

Parents' names _____ Phone# _____

Address _____

Child's name _____ Age _____

Parents' names _____ Phone# _____

Address _____

Child's name _____ Age _____

Parents' names _____ Phone# _____

Address _____

Child's name _____ Age _____

Parents' names _____ Phone# _____

Address _____

Child's name _____ Age _____

Parents' names _____ Phone# _____

Address _____

Child's name _____ Age _____

Parents' names _____ Phone# _____

Address _____

Child's name _____ Age _____

Parents' names _____ Phone# _____

Address _____

Child's name _____ Age _____

Parents' names _____ Phone# _____

Address _____

Child's name _____ Age _____

Parents' names _____ Phone# _____

Address _____

Child's name _____ Age _____

Parents' names _____ Phone# _____

Address _____

Child's name _____ Age _____

Parents' names _____ Phone# _____

Address _____

Child's name _____ Age _____

Parents' names _____ Phone# _____

Address _____

Child's name _____ Age _____

Parents' names _____ Phone# _____

Address _____

ABOUT THE AUTHORS

ELYSE ZORN KARLIN, a freelance writer, is the mother of an eleven-year-old boy who is a budding comedian and magician. She is the author of six books, including one about mothers and sons. She also writes magazine articles and is the editor of a newsletter for a national organization. She has a journalism degree from the University of Missouri School of Journalism.

DAISY SPIER, mother of two, currently heads Spier Research Group, a marketing research firm, and has conducted focus groups with parents throughout the United States. She has a bachelor's degree in psychology from McGill University in Canada, and a master's degree in psychology from Rutgers University.

DIANE PIERCE-WILLIAMS is the mother of three exuberant children ranging from nursery school to high school age. She works both in the home and professionally as an arbitrator. A former single parent and law professor, Diane has a master's degree in communication from the University of Hawaii and a law degree from Harvard University.